SOCIALISM AND PARLIA

# Socialism and Parliamentary Democracy

Geoff Hodgson

Spokesman

First Published in 1977


Paper ISBN 0 85124 200 6
Cloth ISBN 0 85124 207 3



Published by the Bertrand Russell Peace Foundation Ltd., Bertrand Russell House, Gamble Street, Nottingham for *Spokesman*

Printed by the Russell Press Ltd., Nottingham

# Contents

To my parents

# Preface

Two strategic conceptions have dominated the socialist movement since Marx: the parliamentary and the insurrectionary roads to socialism. The former has dominated the routine practice of the British Labour Party and other European socialist and social democratic parties, as well as being tragically put to the test by Allende's Government in Chile in 1970-3. The latter was codified by Lenin and successfully utilised in Russia in 1917. Since then it has remained as the guideline for the Trotskyist movement and other far-left groups. Yet since 1917 neither strategy has succeeded in any advanced capitalist country; by whatever method the socialist transformation has not been accomplished in the West. Attempts at socialist insurrection in Western Europe have failed, and sometimes provoked the reaction of a fascist holocaust. If socialists have attempted by legislation to transform society in a fundamental sense then they have been defeated by either ballot or bullet. Both the insurrectionary and the parliamentary roads, on the basis of all evidence, have turned out to be cul-de-sacs for the West. The unwelcome legacy of this twin failure is the hegemonic strength of right-wing social-democracy, and its consistent acquiescence in the existing capitalist order.

If these facts were driven home then the need for an alternative third road to socialism should be obvious. But the facts of the situation have not been faced by anything but a tiny minority within the socialist movement, and the consequence of this failure of vision has been a deep crisis within every socialist party, group or current. It is a crisis due to both the record of defeat and blindness to the immensity of that defeat. Yet it is my conviction that the crisis can be overcome, and tentative positive moves are already being made in the right direction. In particular a new and sophisticated analysis of the modern epoch is emerging and developing. A second element in the struggle to transform the socialist movement must be the transformation of the very instruments and institutions of that movement. Finally, these elements must combine in a new strategy and perspective for socialist change: a third road to socialism.

A book of this length and calibre cannot be other than a small contribution to the development of this strategy. Its main aim is simply to demonstrate the feasibility and necessity of a third route, without charting out every contour of the terrain, nor detailing every twist in its course, nor designing every necessary construction. The book focusses on the thorny problem of the relation between parliamentary and extra-parliamentary political activity, and argues that a strategic synthesis of actions within each terrain is required.

Such a strategy should be applicable to the advanced capitalist countries of Western Europe: Britain, France, Italy, West Germany and Scandinavia. But clearly there are other countries to which such a dual strategy could be applied, and still others in which an insurrectionary or alternative road will be appropriate. And in every case the details of such a dual strategy will vary from country to country, depending on the precise concrete circumstances: that much is a truism.

The possibility of a third strategy became recently apparent in Chile. Despite the unshaking commitment of Allende, and also the leaders of the Chilean Communist Party, to the parliamentary road: the naive constitutionalism and faith in the loyalty of the armed forces, the very uses to which constitutional and legal methods were put evokes a new vision that will live on after the bloody generals' coup and the death of Allende. For brief moments in their struggle a healthy, mutually reinforcing, dialectic between mass struggle and constitutional reform emerged. But it was limited by the naive constitutionalism of Allende and eventually truncated by the coup. Furthermore, Popular Unity, despite gaining the presidential seat and the formal reins of government, never attained a majority in the legislating Congress, and many of its radical moves were blocked by that body. Chile is a distorted and very limited example of the part-application of a dual strategy of socialist transformation: a strategy that would have a much greater chance of success in an advanced capitalist democracy if lead by a genuine socialist coalition, without narrow parliamentary illusions, but with a necessary majority in Parliament.

It should be evident that our analysis is forced to be somewhat limited and abstract: we must avoid the multitude of concrete details for the time being. It is said in the text that our discussion applies to a country such as Britain. But to mention any specific country brings in numerous important and concrete problems that relate to our analytical domain. We can raise three briefly here in the Preface, and beg the reader's indulgence in their omission from the main text.

The first is the question of national diversification within the United Kingdom – an issue which applies to other European states, e.g. France. The constituent nations of Britain (England, Scotland and Wales in the main) each have a long history of independence and a cultural integrity of their own. Yet through subjugation or sheer bribery they have become dominated by the English ruling class. It would be a chauvinist error, therefore, to regard the territorial bounds of the present Westminster Parliament as inviolable. Devolution, or even national separation, may be a progressive, and even necessary, trauma for the British Isles to endure to undo hundreds of years of colonial and cultural exploitation. The difficulties of restoring national self-determination may even be as great as those connected with the struggle of the Irish for the same goal. But that does not mean that such national and democratic rights can be denied. In consequence, therefore, whilst it is clearly beyond the scope of this work to discuss the thorny problem of devolution and nationalism, and we have confined ourselves to the abstract ground of a static national parliament, this does not deny the important qualifications that a more concrete analysis of the make-up of the British state will bring.

A similar type of problem arises with the question of the European Economic Community. The European Parliament threatens to supersede or dominate the existing parliaments of the member states of the Community, thus pushing all European democratic institutions into a state of change. Whilst it is argued in this book that one necessary aim of socialists in advanced capitalist democracies is to obtain a socialist majority in Parliament, this goal becomes necessary largely because of the historical weight and static nature of national parliaments. In the melting pot of change, with novel institutions, such arguments may not apply. Hence the advocacy of a socialist parliamentary majority cannot be automatically extended to the European Parliament. On the other hand there are strong arguments to support the acceptance of such a goal. The matter can only be decided by a more concrete and extended discussion: again beyond the scope of this work.

Thirdly, it is well-recognised that the British state apparatus contains many feudalistic and non-democratic appendages, such as the House of Lords and the monarchy. The word Parliament, in the British context, sometimes connotes such outdated institutions. To avoid confusion, therefore, we refer to Parliament in the abstract and exclusive sense of a democratically elected body, i.e. in Britain the House of Commons, without the Lords and the monarchy. The necessary reforms of the state apparatus to which we refer in the text must, of course, include the abolition of all inherited political power and privilege, and the assertion of the goal of a socialist republic.

It is opportune in a preface such as this to anticipate some possible responses to this work by its critics. No doubt it will be seen by some as 'reformist'. But the careful reader will note that the need for a fundamental and decisive transfer of political power, something beyond the bounds of linear and gradualistic change, is advocated. It is clear that this book suggests that democratic forms do have some supra-class content, and there is not a Chinese Wall between 'bourgeois' and 'proletarian' democracy, as Lenin insisted. Yet despite the fact that Marx himself makes no such hard and fast distinction between two forms of modern democracy some critics will accuse me of regarding the entire state apparatus as neutral. Again the careful reader will note that this is a *non sequitur.* In fact such critics would fall into the error of identifying the nature of democratic forms with the nature of the state itself. The author remains convinced of the general Marxist principle of the non-neutrality and class-bias of the state, even though the precise articulation of the state and class structures is more complex than is suggested in much vulgar Marxist literature.

This work is at variance with the particular Marxist tradition that stretches from Lenin to

Trotsky. But a number of qualifications are necessary. First, the variance is primarily due to the fact that their strategic conceptions were designed, consciously or unconsciously, for autocratic Eastern Europe in the experience of the Russian Revolution. And in that context they were a major and largely applicable achievement. The mistake comes in their wholesale application to the West. The distinct features of the western capitalist democracies necessitate a new supra-Leninist strategy. Second, however, this does not deny many of the major valuable additions that both Lenin and Trotsky have made to Marxism: in the former case a methodology of revolutionary action, a theory of imperialism and national self-determination, and a legitimate and universal emphasis on the need for mass struggle; in the latter case a brilliant analysis of fascism and a forceful critique of Stalinism, amongst other things, were added.

As this work still claims to reside within the Marxist tradition as a whole then the reader may wish to compare it with other Marxist forerunners. Bernstein, Kautsky or Gramsci may come to mind. A comment on each of these may be appropriate. The *Prison Notebooks* had an enormous influence on me in the period 1971-3 in which time I was finalising my ideological break from the politics of the far-left. Despite the many obscurities and ambiguities in Gramsci's work it has been a monumental influence. The same cannot be said for the other two forementioned socialists. In my view Bernstein is the inferior of the two and has been ably criticised in Colletti's book *From Rousseau to*

*Lenin*. The case of Kautsky is more problematic. He has few friends on the Marxist left these days, yet his political position is remarkably close to that of present-day Communist Parties. He deserves to be discussed in a more informed climate, devoid of the Pavlovian response of immediate condemnation on sound of his name. On the surface, some of his strategic conceptions were close to those in his book. Yet in content the divergencies are greater. For Kautsky mass struggle almost always had parliament as its focus; his advocacy of additional mass institutions was limited to say the least. (The same criticism can be made of the Communist Parties today). Kautsky correctly perceived the difficulties of applying a purely Leninist strategy west of the Vistula. Yet this observation was eventually formulated as a blanket and near-total condemnation of the Bolsheviks and the Third International in both East and West. Without the sharpness of mind of Lenin, Trotsky or Gramsci, Kautsky became a victim of his own turbulent period. The events of his time, and the new epoch that was wrought, exceeded the compass of his analytical capabilities even more than the other three. After 1919 he relapsed into crude Bernsteinian reformism. Yet he has still made many positive contributions to Marxism which deserve much more than their present ostracization.

In addition to the work of Antonio Gramsci, I wish to record the influences of living writers such as Perry Anderson, Lucio Colletti, Gareth Stedman Jones and Ralph Miliband. Ken Coates, apart from being another valuable influence, has given me encouragement to complete this work; for which I am grateful. Finally, I wish to thank my friend and political colleague, Peter Jenkins. Over the years that we have worked together and shared the same political trajectory and experience, Peter has shared in the discussion and formulation of many of the ideas of the book, and at times has been an indispensable critic. I hope that he will notice some of his intellectual handiwork on these pages, for which he is acknowledged with gratitude, and not wish to disassociate himself from too much of its remaining content.

*Geoff Hodgson*
*August 1977*

# Socialism and Parliamentary Democracy

> "the first step in the revolution by the working class is to raise the proletariat to the position of ruling class, to win the battle of democracy"
>
> *Marx and Engels,* Manifesto of the Communist Party

## *Introduction*

It is the aim of this essay to explore a theme which is becoming ever-more topical at the present time: the potentialities and limitations of parliamentary democracy. The issue has surfaced in national papers such as the *Guardian.* It has been the subject of a somewhat muffled, but nevertheless consequential, debate in the Communist Party. The reverberations have now even spread to some sections of the Trotskyist left. It has been rare in the past for such a theoretical issue to be debated in such a wide arena.

Of course, there are reasons for this. We can name a few. Increasing tension within the Labour Party, on the issue of the implementation of genuinely socialist policies, and on the question of the right of Trotskyists and other Marxists to remain within the Party, has led this issue to be raised, amongst others. The slow winds of change are being felt within the Communist Party, particularly as a result of the changes of position of the French and Italian Communist Parties on the very question of attitudes to democratic institutions within developed capitalist societies. The failure of soviet-type bodies, or workers' councils, to appear and sustain themselves in capitalist democracies in Europe or North America has began to generate some self-critical thinking within some of the Trotskyist groups. These groups mushroomed in Britain around 1968, but they all have been at a bewildered loose-end for a decade, due to the failure of the French events of May 1968 to repeat themselves in any advanced capitalist nation.

This essay is intended as a contribution to socialist strategy. It must be made clear, however, that we do not refer to parliamentary institutions *in general.* We are to concern ourselves mainly with the question of the socialist transformation in Britain, and with the nature and function of the British Parliament in particular. We are quite prepared to concede that the following analysis does not apply to some countries: particularly those without a long tradition of parliamentary democracy.

## *Six Propositions Affirmed*

Before we construct our main argument it would be useful, to give some indication of our standpoint, to affirm six basic and highly important propositions. For those which dispute some or all of them, some reasons for their acceptance and affirmation will be given below.

1. The parliamentary apparatus has, on its own, little effective power for fundamental social change.

2. The transition to a fully socialist society requires struggle and direct involvement by the mass of the population, and the creation of many directly representative democratic institutions at the grass roots level.

3. The transition to socialism may involve military or other conflict. Even if it does not, in any case the socialist movement must remove the threat of armed counter-revolution, coup d'etat, or sabotage by the police force or armed services.

4. Even when a socialist regime is established it must protect itself against the possibility of counter-revolution or sabotage by an internal minority, or by invasion from outside. In other words, in these circumstances, it must protect its power by force.

5. In a developed industrial society a socialist regime cannot develop effectively on the basis of parliamentary democracy alone. A mass participative democracy is required, including, for example, workers' control at the point of production.

6. The nationally elected body of representatives in a socialist society, whether it retains the title of "parliament" or not, must be constituted in such a way that the representatives are under direct recall by those that elected them and do not receive excessive renumeration for the office.

Regarding the first proposition, Miliband, in his excellent book *Parliamentary Socialism*, has chronicled and analysed the failures of those who have attempted to use Parliament, on its own, for socialist change. Illusions in the power of an individual Member of Parliament, or in the power of the Parliamentary Labour Party have in the past been reincarnated and dashed, time and time again. Such is the despairing saga of parliamentary socialism. Miliband's analysis gives support to the second proposition above. Parliament on its own cannot accomplish fundamental change, so the struggle and creativity of the working people must be utilised. Historical experience confirms this. No capitalist system has been destroyed without the involvement and efforts of the masses. Even when the Soviet Union created regimes in Eastern Europe after the defeat of the Nazis, which, at most, were socialist regimes of a degenerate and undemocratic sort, working class power had to be utilised to accomplish the social transformation.

The experience of the catastrophe of the violent overthrow of the Allende regime in Chile is fresh in our minds. This should confirm the third proposition, and remind us that socialists must always be aware of the possibility of violent reaction or resistance to their progress, even if that socialist progress has the support of the majority of the population. These possibilities must be kept in mind, and prepared for, both in agitation and action. Quite obviously, a socialist regime must budget for its own defence, and protect itself against invasion, or threat of reactionary force from within. Any realistic politician must accept this. Nevertheless, if socialists have to use force it is always with regret. And if force can be avoided then so much the better.

Whether or not force is actually used will depend upon the use or avoidance of force, or the threat of force, by those opposed to socialism.

Regarding the fifth and sixth propositions we cannot give them full argumentation here. We must simply state that in a complex industrial society mass democracy is an economic and social necessity for the full development of that society in the interests of its members. In addition, it is always necessary to be vigilant and aware of any possible tendency towards bureaucratisation and the development of an elite. For the latter reason the principle of direct recall and accountability of all elected representatives is necessary. They should not be able to entrench their power through patronage or nepotism, nor should they receive excessive payment for their services.

### *Seven Propositions to be Proved*

To make our political position clear we have affirmed, without rigorous demonstration, six propositions in the foregoing section. We now come to the purpose of this chapter. We intend to construct strong arguments to support the following seven propositions:

7. The term "bourgeois democracy" is highly misleading and it should not be applied to Parliament, as such, in Britain.

8. In advanced capitalist democracies parliaments do have some power, of a sort, and they are not merely a facade.

9. As part of the process of achieving a socialist transformation a genuinely socialist party must aim to achieve an elected majority of its members in the existing parliament.

10. Socialists should not aim at a destruction of parliament nor a smashing of parliamentary institutions.

11. A national congress of delegates from soviet-type bodies should not be the *supreme* decision-making body in a socialist regime in Britain, even if soviets and a congress of soviet representatives are desirable. (By a soviet we mean, of course, a council of worker representatives elected from the work-places in a particular district).

12. The supreme decision-making body in a socialist regime in Britain should be some sort of parliament, based, essentially, on universal adult franchise.

13. All socialists, Marxist or otherwise, do not aid the cause of socialism in Britain by continuing to use the term "dictatorship of the proletariat" whatever the users of that term may take it to mean.

To some, it may appear at first sight that propositions 1 to 6 are logically inconsistent with 7 to 13. However, on close inspection, it will be evident that there is no logical inconsistency. For example, to say in 1 that parliaments have, *on their own,* little effective power, is not inconsistent with subsequent statements that parliament should be utilised and maintained. For if parliament is *supplemented* by mass activity and grass roots institutions then the *combined* power of all these institutions can, indeed, be highly effective. Apparent inconsistencies can arise due to certain outdated and invalid frameworks of thought that exist on the socialist left. Having found no logical inconsistency, the basis and substantiation of the latter seven propositions can now be examined.

*Evaluative Criteria*

We cannot claim to provide a complete proof or substantiation of the seven propositions. Such proofs are rarely possible in political theory. In any case, if the seven propositions are to be firmly verified then it will only be in the very practice of creating a socialist society. In politics the ultimate criteria of proof are always related to practice.

This essay is mainly written for socialists. Thus one initial premise can probably be agreed: that socialism is both possible and desirable, more desirable than any other feasible economic system for the time being. It may be suggested by some that socialism is also inevitable, but that does not have to be raised here. If socialism is possible and desirable then we can direct our attention towards the *means* of attaining that agreed end. By socialism, of course, we mean a society with collective ownership and democratic control of the bulk of the means of production.

It should be clear, therefore, that our strategic propositions are not based, fundamentally, on *other* moral principles. Advocation or rejection of strategic imperatives is related to the prime objective of creating a socialist society.

However, on one point, we must make it clear that in a developed industrial society socialism must be based on extensive and powerful democratic institutions. There is no socialism without democracy. Furthermore, the advancement and advocacy of socialism in Britain must necessarily involve the advancement and advocacy of mass democracy. Quite different strategic guidelines applied, for example, to a less developed capitalist country such as Russia in the early decades of this century.

From our premise that socialism is both possible and desirable we can deduce a general criterion to assess all strategic imperatives. The criterion is this: *effectiveness in moving towards and creating socialism.* In other words, a strategic imperative is judged according to the criterion of whether or not it is estimated, on the basis of a scientific analysis of the developing situation, that the implementation of the strategic imperative would actually further the creation of socialism. Our argument in favour of the seven propositions, therefore, is based upon the estimation that their implementation is necessary in order to achieve a socialist society in Britain.

For the purpose of our argument we need not, incidentally, take a position as to whether or not socialism can develop in one country. Our argument is not affected substantially by that issue. We can acknowledge, however, that the pursuance of socialism in Britain is very likely to be aided considerably by socialist developments in other major countries, especially those in Western Europe.

## *Democracy and "Bourgeois Democracy"*

We shall address ourselves at first to proposition 7. Is it legitimate to use the term "bourgeois democracy" in Britain? It was Lenin who popularised the term, particularly in his *Proletarian Revolution and the Renegade Kautsky.* In this work Lenin gives a forceful account of the limitations of "bourgeois democracy": its subjection to the interests of the capitalists, its closed and secretive nature, its failure to enlist the mass of the population in decision-making and administration, and so on. These observations still apply to the British Parliament, and other parliaments, and relate to issues which are absolutely vital and central to the question of transforming society. In contrast, according to Lenin, "proletarian democracy" overcomes these severe limitations by basing itself on soviet-type bodies which "are the direct organisations of the working and exploited people themselves". A soviet "*helps* them to organise and administer their own state in every possible way".

But this sharp division between "proletarian" and "bourgeois" democracy is misleading and unsatisfactory, for a number of reasons. First, the limitations of "bourgeois democracy" are not *necessarily* connected to the *form* of "bourgeois democracy", i.e. parliament. It would be absurd to situations and forms of society, e.g. medieval situations and forms of society, e.g. mediaeval England, the seventeenth-century Commonwealth, semi-absolutist pre-1918 Germany, pre-revolutionary Russia, and so on. Can we claim that the more important factor is the *form* of parliamentary democracy and not its structural relation to the particular social system involved? Of course not. Could we suggest that if a parliament did exist in a socialist society then the power of the capitalists would be augumented or restored, and government would automatically become secretive and exclude the masses from power? Of course not. As long as mass institutions of popular power still existed, and the *military* power of the capitalist class had been smashed then there would be no reason to assume that the existence of parliament would *automatically* lead to such a degeneration or capitalist restoration. Lenin's distinction does not take sufficient account of the distinction between the form and content of parliamentary democracy.

Second, Lenin gives no reason why the form of parliamentary democracy cannot be improved substantially in a socialist society, and connected with a system of mass popular government which did help the people to "organise and administer their own state in every possible way". In other words, Lenin gives no *general* reason why parliament has to be abolished under a socialist regime, even if their were sufficient reasons to abolish the Russian Constituent Assembly under threat of civil war, in a society with no established tradition of parliamentary democracy. We cannot agree with Kautsky's abstract and moralistic attack on the revolutionary Soviet regime in his book *The Dictatorship of the Proletariat,* of which Lenin's forementioned pamphlet was a critique. But both Lenin and Kautsky made the serious mistake of constructing their assessments of parliamentary democracy and Soviet power in general terms, rather than by assessing the Bolshevik regime in particular.

Although Marx, himself, never constructed an adequate theory of political action, and Lenin's contribution in this field was by far the greater, Marx was more cautious in his assessment of particular regimes. As far as this author is aware Marx only once, in 1879, uses the term "bourgeois democracy". Furthermore, on the few occasions on which Marx talks of smashing state institutions in a proletarian revolution he never clearly states that parliament, *in general,* has to be smashed. Reference to the Paris Commune is not really relevant on this issue, for unfortunately it was a proletarian insurrection confined to one besieged city, and there was no possibility of calling a representative parliament from within the seige. The Commune was a municipal rather than a national insurrection (one reason, of course, why it was defeated). The adoption of the term "commune" by the Paris insurgents was not due to any communist sympathies but to the fact that it is the traditional French, Spanish and Italian term for "municipality". In a letter dated 12 April 1871, written to Kugelmann at the very time of the Paris Commune, Marx wrote the famous words:

> If you look up the last chapter of my *Eighteenth Brumaire* you will find that I declare that the next attempt of the French Revolution will be no longer, as before, to transfer the bureaucratic-military machine from one hand to another, but to *smash* it, and this is the precondition for every real people's revolution on the Continent.

There are two important qualifications in the above sentence which are not often emphasised. First, Marx is talking about "people's revolution on the Continent", so there is the *possibility* that he did not regard his prescription as directly or completely applicable to Britain. Even more important is the second qualification: Marx does not talk of smashing the state in its entirety but only of the bureaucratic-military machine. Hence he does not state that, in general, parliaments have to be smashed. We cannot agree, however, that, in general, all bureaucracies have to be smashed. But we can certainly agree that, in general, the means of reactionary military repression have to be smashed, and we have stated this much in propositions 3 and 4 above.

Regarding this vital topic of democracy and state power the works of Marx, Engels and Lenin contain ambiguities, inconsistencies and sometimes errors. For too long debate on this issue has simply consisted of the firing of quotation and counter-quotation. Whilst the works of Marx, Engels and Lenin are exceedingly useful on this topic they cannot be regarded as the source of all truth. After all, in the times before the First World War, only a few major countries, such as France and the United States, operated a uniform franchise where more than one-third of the adult population were allowed to vote. In Britain, for example, in 1914 only 30 per cent of the adult population over the age of 20 years, had the vote, as there was a property qualification and women were disenfranchised. As Göran Therborn points out in a recent issue of *New Left Review*, if full democracy is defined to exclude all racial, sexual or class disqualifications then the attainment of that goal is relatively recent. Full democracy was instituted in Britain in 1928, Germany in 1919 (later to be abolished by the Nazis and reinstituted after the war), France and Italy in 1946, and the United States as late as the 1970s. On the whole, full democracy is a post Second World War phenomenon. Even Lenin and Trotsky did not live to see the flowering of democracy in the West. Can we injudiciously use the term "bourgeois democracy" and ignore the electoral and structural changes that have occured in parliamentary democracy, in this country and elsewhere, in the last sixty years? It seems that we should not.

### *Parliamentary and "Proletarian" Democracy*

No doubt it would be difficult to construct the features of what Lenin called "proletarian democracy" through the normal process of parliamentary legislation. But that does not mean that parliament has to be smashed in order to achieve a workers' democracy: with mass popular involvement in the administration, elected representatives under recall, etc. There is no reason, in principle, why it should not be possible to modify the constitution so that Members of Parliament are subject to the recall of their constitutents. We may have to await the formation of a genuine socialist government before such a reform is possible. But there is no reason to suppose that it is impossible, especially *after* the creation of additional mass organs of democratic control, and the breaking of the military and economic power of the capitalist class. It seems that "proletarian democracy" does not, in principle, exclude parliamentary democracy, despite Lenin's rebuttal of the latter.

It is, of course, necessary for socialists to emphasise the narrowness and limitations of parliamentary democracy. The struggle for workers' control, workers' councils, and other grass-roots institutions is absolutely essential. But these struggles do not necessarily exclude the struggle to reform parliament so that it is less and less able to serve the interests of the bourgeoisie whom, after all, constitute a very small fraction of the electorate. Such a struggle, to improve parliamentary democracy in the interests of the working class, has a long and proud history in Britain. It formed the basis of the demands of the Chartists, in the last century. Working class mobilisation played its part in the attempts to widen the franchise in the 1860s and after. In part, therefore, parliamentary democracy in Britain has been modified and improved by working-class pressure. The hard Leninist division between "bourgeois" and "proletarian" democracy seems to support the view that the working class movement, after 150 years of intense struggle, should knock down that which that they have a hand in building, and start afresh with something new. It is like asking a man to demolish his imperfect dwelling and then suffer the risk of no protection from the elements whilst something new is put in its place. In reality the risk is the one of reactionary dictatorship. Why not, at least, build the new dwelling before the old one is condemned?

It is not surprising that orthodox Leninism has never gained significant roots in any developed capitalist democracy.

However, our argument that parliamentary democracy is not necessarily the exclusive preserve of bourgeois class interests should not be taken to imply that the state, as a whole, is a neutral class vessel into which different political class interests can be poured. Contrary to social-democratic myth, the state is *not* neutral. Neither is parliament an institution which, in a given class society, can be neutral, above classes, nor fully reflect the interests of the majority. Our point is simply that parliament is not *necessarily* connected to bourgeois class rule, even if it may usually reflect bourgeois class interests (despite universal suffrage). It follows from this point that the existence of some form of extended and reformed parliamentary democracy is possible under socialism, and that parliament does not have to be smashed in order to complete the socialist transformation. But that does not mean that vast institutional changes in the nature of democracy are not required. Furthermore, as we have stated above, the repressive agencies of the bourgeois state will have to be smashed, and countless other fundamental changes in the state apparatus will have to be made.

## *Is Parliament a "Facade"?*

In proposition 1 it was asserted that, on its own, parliament has little effective power. With that in mind we now turn to a substantiation of proposition 8.

The key words are "on its own". An example of the limitation of parliamentary power when it is not supplemented by effective executive institutions at the grass-roots is the fate of recent factory legislation improving health and safety conditions at work. On this vital reform it has been impossible to implement legal standards as yet, due to the limited numbers of factory inspectors and the weakness of the factory inspectorate. The legal standards will probably not be fully implemented until the trade unions take upon themselves some of the major powers of a factory inspector. Legislation, by itself, has not brought the necessary reforms.

To be fully effective, most significant legislation must be backed up by some powerful executive body. In many cases, of course, the body which translates parliamentary legislation into effective law is the police force. The existence of the police in itself is a deterrent to breaking the law. The courts and prisons also have their role. But in general, leaving aside some notable and scandalous exceptions, the police and law courts would not have power to deter, arrest and punish on a particular issue, without the necessary parliamentary legislation. We can conclude that parliament does, therefore, have some civil power, even if that power has to be combined with bodies like the police and law courts in order to be effective. Both the police and law courts, on the one hand, and the legislative process in parliament, on the other, have to depend upon each other in order to be fully effective in a parliamentary democracy.

But few laws are implemented on threat of arrest or punishment alone. A significant factor lying behind adherence to the law in developed capitalist democracies is the *consent* of the population at large. It is not the case, of course, that many people have a hand in framing and legislating the various laws, neither do all laws rest upon the agreement of the majority of the population. But it is the case, however, that most people believe that the main assembly which passes legal legislation, i.e. parliament, does in some indirect way reflect or respond to the wishes of the majority. This belief may be unfounded, but it is a belief which, for various historical and social reasons, prevails nevertheless.

A crucial theoretical task for socialists, therefore, is to study and understand the processes and structures which generate this mass consent. It would be beyond the scope of this essay to attempt such an analysis here. Important work has been done on this in the past, particularly by Perry Anderson in his two essays in the volume *Towards Socialism,* and by Ralph Miliband in his *State in Capitalist Society.* It cannot be contested, on the basis of an adequate study of the structures of political power in Britain, that Parliament does play a vital and central role in the generation of that mass consent.

It is not simply due to the fact that people believe that Paliament is partially or wholly representative. It is a deeper and more complex process. Beliefs, ideologies, and elements of consciousness are not simply illusions lurking in the shadows of the mind, out of the glare of a contrasting reality. Institutions, such as parliament, are more like lenses and prisms which focus life experience under capitalism onto a particular plane of understanding and action. To take a simple example, the strong refractive powers of parliamentary institutions in Britain, tend to divert struggles over wages and conditions onto the electoral and parliamentary terrain. This, in turn, changes the character and direction of those struggles and moulds the very consciousness of the participants in struggle. At least, therefore, it must be admitted that parliament, as a longstanding and central institution, has a tremendous power to mould working class conceptions and divert elemental struggles into its ordained channels.

The creation of mass consent is aided by parliament because of its capacity to construct the social cognition of reality in its own terms. Struggles and issues get diverted towards the parliamentary terrain and this becomes recognised and endorsed as the legitimate arena of decision, arbitration, and legislation. To some, this process may seem unfortunate and overwhelming but it must be recognised and assessed for what it is. It would be a highly dangerous mistake not to do this, and instead substitute our conception of what we think *ought* to be.

To re-state our point, therefore, parliament is not merely a facade; it has a strong power to structure consciousness and manufacture mass consent. It is now convenient to consider some important examples, which also support propositions 9 and 10.

### *The Defeat of the German Revolution of 1918-19*

At the end of the First World War the German nation seemed at the point of collapse. The years of slaughter in the trenches, and shortages at home, had bled the nation white. The German war-machine came to a halt. In the army and navy, mutiny followed mutiny, until, in the revolutionary explosion of 9 November 1918, the Kaiser abdicated and the old imperial German monarchy came to an end. The vacuum in government was immediately filled by a six-man "Council of People's Commissioners"; three were right-wing social democrats and three were left-wing "Independent" socialists. At the time the right-wing had already started to communicate and collaborate with certain reactionary elements in the fragmented Germany army, but the left was not aware of these closely-guarded secret agreements. The right-wing social-democrats had no intention of creating anything more than a parliamentary democratic bourgeois republic. The left of the council, members of the Independent Social-Democratic Party, wished to establish authentic socialism in Germany. Outside the Council, the Spartacists, led by Karl Liebknecht and Rosa Luxemburg, had the intention of fomenting a proletarian revolution on the model of the Bolshevik insurrection of a year earlier. The Independents and Spartacists had the support of only a few per cent of the urban working class, whilst the right-wing social-democrats had at least the tacit support of probably the majority of the working class.

On the early morning of 10 November the six-man Council called a delegate meeting of the workers and soldiers of Berlin. Three thousand of these delegates assembled in the afternoon, in radical and revolutionary mood. Fraternal greetings were sent to the "Russian Workmen's and Soldiers'

Government". The immediate nationalization of German industry was demanded. Then, more to the interests of the right-wing, the six-man Council was ratified by acclamation. An additional twenty-eight man "Executive Council of the Berlin Workers' and Soldiers' Councils" was elected. Its membership was almost equally divided between Independents and right-wing social democrats. Despite their vocal presence at the meeting not a single Spartacist managed to get elected. The "Executive Council" saw one of its tasks as calling a *national* congress of representatives of the workers' and soldiers' councils which had been, and were being, set up in most areas of Germany. In practice, however, the six-man Council conducted the nation's affairs. They enacted some significant legislation, establishing the eight-hour day, guaranteeing the right of trade-union organisation in the factories, raising sick, old-age, and unemployment benefits, abolishing censorship of the press, and releasing political prisoners.

In the meantime the Spartacists were impatient. Luxemburg emphasised the weakness of their working class support and urged caution, but the remainder, led by Liebknecht, agitated for the immediate overthrow of the six-man Council. Soviet authorities supported this action, broadcasting a radio message urging the continuation of the revolution: a government of workers' councils must be set up under the leadership of Liebknecht. Throughout November the Spartacists seized every opportunity to harass the government and promote civil war. Their actions at least managed to increase the polarisation of the six-man Council between right and left, but the Spartacists did not sufficiently increase their mass support – they remained a small minority.

On 16 December a National Congress of Workers' and Soldiers' Councils began in Berlin, its purpose being to transfer political sovereignty over Germany to a national group, as distinguished from the Berlin workers' and soldiers' councils. About 60 per cent of the delegates were from the right-wing social-democrats, who forced through a resolution calling for a general election on 19 January. The elected parliament would then draft a constitution and be the sovereign body of the German Republic.

The right-wing social democrats no doubt saw the election as partly a device to undermine the influence of the workers' and soldiers' councils, and for that reason they directed every effort towards that goal. The Sparticists suspected this ploy, and had little enthusiasm for any national assembly based on anything else but the workers' and soldiers' councils. It became their objective not only to break up the forthcoming elections and prevent the convening of a parliament, but also to break up the National Congress of Workers' and Soldiers' Councils which was in the process of approving a new parliamentary democracy. The Spartacist rationale for disregarding the decisions of the National Congress was their belief that it was fraudulently packed by the right.

The methods they used to break up the National Congress were amazing. R. M. Watt, in his book *The Kings Depart,* describes the scene as follows:

> For the five dishevelled days (16-20 December) that the congress met, Liebknecht and his followers turned it into a bedlam. Some seven thousand Spartacists gathered outside . . . and the noise of their catcalls and hoots could clearly be heard inside. From time to time Spartacists burst into the meeting, shouted slogans, exhortations and threats, then dashed out of the exits. Others paraded up and down the aisles carrying placards . . . groups of armed sailors of the People's Naval Division charged into the hall. They had daubed their faces with mud, and the effect was as startling as they could have wished. Waving their rifles, they demanded that a true Red Guard be formed immediately, that plans for a National Assembly (parliament) be abandoned, and that the system of government by the workers' and soldiers' councils be perpetuated. (pp. 256-7)

The Spartacist agitation had some effect, but naturally it did not win the congress over to their views. In fact it tended to polarise the delegates between the strategies of pure insurrection, on the one hand, and narrow parliamentarianism, on the other.

Rosa Luxemburg had a more sophisticated conception. At a congress to form the Communist Party of Germany on December 30 a major portion of time was given over to the question of elections and the proposed new parliament. Luxemburg and Levi argued that the party should participate in the elections, but this view was lost, and by a large majority it was decided on a boycott.

During the first week of January 1919 huge strikes and riots became a daily occurrence. On 5 January the Communists, left-wing Independents, and Revolutionary Shop Stewards, met together to discuss the issue of a sacked Berlin police chief. Startingly, Liebknecht carried a decision to start an armed revolution the following day. So the "Spartacist Revolution" began. A general strike brought Berlin to a standstill, and armed workers seized strategic buildings.

A few days earlier the Spartacist organisation had changed its name to the Communist Party of Germany. However, only Liebknecht and one other Communist had attended the 5 January meeting. As to the rest of the leadership, Watt writes:

> Rosa Luxemburg, Leo Jogiches and Karl Radek had been appalled when they learned that the 5 January conference of the parties of the left had decided to proclaim the revolution. They were not alone. The majority of the party's *Zentrale* was similarly horrified. They saw quite clearly that the proletarian movement was not yet ready for a real revolution, and they cursed the luck which had permitted Liebknecht to go almost alone to the meeting . . . The masses were not yet properly educated. The thing which Rose Luxemburg had most feared, a premature uprising of the proletariat, had occurred . . . Agitation and propoganda were both well short of their goals. Even if this uprising succeeded – and Luxemburg was sure it would not – it could be sustained only by Leninist policies of terror. (pp. 296-7)

Only the week before, Luxemburg had written:

> It would be a criminal error to seize power now. The German working class is not ready for such an act . . . It is useless, it is childish to overthrow it (the social-democratic government) and replace it by another if the masses are not ready and able to organize Germany. (R. Fischer, *Stalin and German Communism,* p. 74).

Although Radek argued that the uprising must be stopped, even disarmed, Luxemburg and the other leaders felt that the Party could not now abandon the workers. As doomed as the revolution may be, they must mix its fate with theirs. So it was to be.

On 11 January the *Freikorps* entered inner Berlin. By 15 January the revolution had been bloodily crushed and the city was in their hands. That night both Liebknecht and Luxemburg were captured. Liebknecht was shot whilst "attempting to escape". Luxemburg had her brains blown out and her corpse was thrown into a canal.

Four days later, according to schedule, the general election was held. The right-wing social-democrats obtained nearly 40 per cent of the vote, by far the largest of any single party. The Independents received only 7 per cent. The Communists boycotted the election. In the wake of the "Spartacist Week" the bourgeois parties managed to stage a remarkable recovery. The social-democrats asked the left-wing Independents to join a government, demanding that the Independents agree to the principles of parliamentary democracy and renounce support for another insurrection. The Independents refused, and the social-democrats found allies to the right, amongst the bourgeois parties. The Weimar Republic was born.

### *The Relevance of the Experience of the German Revolution*

The contemporary myth on the left is that the German revolution of 1918-19 conformed in essential detail to the events in Russia in 1917, with the exception that the German "October" ended in defeat for the revolutionaries. In fact, the differences amount to much more than that, and an analysis of the contrasts can lead to some essential strategic guidelines for today.

In the first place, unlike the situation before the October Revolution in Russia, the revolutionaries never obtained majority support in the workers' councils in Germany. And, as we have seen, they attempted to break up a congress of those councils. In contrast, Lenin and the Bolsheviks saw the achievement of majority support in the soviets as a precondition for insurrection. In fact, in Petersburg, the rising was carried out in the very name of the soviets. It *may* have been impossible to obtain such a revolutionary majority in the German councils, due to social-democratic manipulation and so on. But in that case the revolutionaries should at least have drawn the conclusion that an insurrection was doomed to defeat.

Then two further questions arise. Should the Spartacists have attempted to sabotage the general election as they did? And could they have won over a majority in the workers' councils on the basis of such intransigent contempt for parliamentary democracy? Despite severe limitations and distortions pre-war Germany did have some tradition of parliamentary democracy, more so than Russia. Also the focus of social-democratic strategy in the pre-war period had been the goal of a parliamentary majority. It was not surprising, therefore, that, on the whole, the German working class had some allegiance to parliamentary democracy. Once the Kaiser had been overthrown they naturally saw the next step as the creation of a liberal and egalitarian parliamentary republic. Due to social and political traditions in stark contrast to Russia, the German working class inclined toward parliamentarianism and rejected insurrection. Some may argue that it was necessary to change that situation. But, in any case, it would not be easy to sweep away such embedded notions and traditions. They certainly would not be swept away by a hopeless insurrection which did not even have the support of the workers' councils. Neither would a worker, captured by the illusions of social-democracy, be inclined to abandon the seemingly feasible project of a liberal parliamentary republic, and follow the line of those who wanted workers' councils to rule but tried to sabotage the very decisions and actions of those workers' councils.

In contrast, in Russia the Bolsheviks won the support of the majority of the urban proletariat by such tactics as the united front to smash Kornilov in August 1917. They allied with the Provisional Government, Mensheviks, and others. The result was not only Kornilov's defeat but the demonstration, *in action,* of the necessity of mass action by the working class. If we transfer the principle of a united front to the German situation the conclusion must be this: first, the Spartacists should have worked within the workers' councils with the aim of maintaining their armed existence, even under social democratic domination and manipulation, with the partial object of preparing for any *coup* by monarchists or reactionary *Freikorps.* Secondly, given that successful insurrection was not on the cards, this meant temporary support for the six-man Council, as Lenin gave temporary support to the Provisional Government at certain times during 1917. Third, the Spartacists should not have attempted to sabotage but participated in the parliamentary elections. Whilst doing this they could have pointed out the limitations of a parliament and campaigned for *parliamentary legitimation* and support for armed workers' councils. They could have proposed a republic in which the workers' councils had legitimate authority and effective power, and were capable of influencing a still existing but transformed parliament. Such proposals would have been capable of capturing the support of the social-democratic masses in the workers' councils, and challenged the hegemony of the right.

One consequence of such a strategy would have been that it would have been more difficult to use the *Freikorps* against the workers. On several occasions the *Freikorps* proved vulnerable to mass agitation by the workers. Spartacist agitation would have been ten times more effective if they had tolerated, and participated in, the new parliament, and postponed their insurrection. The *Freikorps* could not have marched and fought with the exclusive claim to represent parliamentary democracy, and they would have been more prone to defection and mutiny.

We do not state, however, that such a strategy would have been easy to follow or assured of success. But it appears that there was little effective alternative. Supporters of the purely insurrectionary road to socialism are very fond of quoting "historical proof" of their strategy. The fact of the matter is that, in history, neither a purely insurrectionary nor a purely parliamentary strategy have *ever* succeeded in an advanced capitalist democracy. The tragic impotence of purely insurrectionary tactics was never more graphically illustrated than in Germany in 1918-19.

### *The Revolt in France, May 1968*

The remarkable revival of the revolutionary left in Western Europe in the last decade is largely due to the tremendous events in France in May, and early June, 1968. In particular, one impact of these events has been to resuscitate the view of a purely insurrectionary road to socialism in Western Europe. From being an unfulfilled hope in the post-war developed capitalist world, a dream near-smothered in the mist of quiet despair, the insurrectionary road to socialism became brightly illuminated by the street-battles, the massive and unprecedented strikes, and the pangs of a Gaullist regime struggling for survival. Or so it seemed – to those of us who filled the streets of the cities and chanted: "We shall fight, we shall win: Paris, London, then Berlin!".

But the French events did not reach insurrectionary proportions, neither did London or Berlin follow that road. The "Hot Autumn" in Italy 1969 may have appeared as "May 1968 in slow-motion" but its movement was fragmentary and somewhat disparate. May 1968 gave a massive boost to the revolutionary left in Western Europe. But as time went on, and the flames of the revolt receded into the distance, the left seemed to be basing all its conceptions on the simple hope of a repetition of the events. A movement was created by 1968, but in the absence of real developments to mirror its expectations it was disposed to base its strategy on faith. Some writers have tended to argue that May 1968 happened as a result of peculiar and unique circumstances. They may be right, but we shall not discuss that question here. It is more unusual, and equally useful, to question why the revolt lost its momentum after attaining such massive proportions. We shall show that even if such events can be repeated they will, of necessity, force us to look the question of parliamentary democracy in the eye. For one hidden lesson of May 1968 is that parliamentary democracy has a weight and significance that cannot be ignored. The view that parliaments are a "facade" does not square up with the reality of the 1968 revolt. If such institutions were so paper-thin then they would have been blown away in the rising wind of revolution.

First came the street battles in the Latin Quarter. Then the "Night of the Barricades" of 10-11 May, providing a spark which leapt from the students to the working class of France. From mid-May to mid-June the French economy was paralysed by a historically unprecedented mass strike. Nearly ten million workers stopped work. Many factories were occupied. In the town of Nantes the strike developed into a seizure of municipal power; a committee of workers, peasants and students became the real local authority. Yet, by the end of

June, it was all over. Not unexpectedly, the state's use of force and the threat of force played its part in suppressing the French revolt. But, apart from several notable deaths and injuries, the revolt was not drowned in blood. Unlike the Paris Commune of 1871, where no less than twenty thousand people were massacred by reactionary forces, at most a few dozen workers and students lost their lives in May and June. The strange paradox is this: that despite its massive popular and active support the May revolt was suppressed not so much by the exercise of force by the capitalist state but by the manipulated "consent" of those very masses themselves. The strike was ended because the masses were presented with no other evident realistic alternative than a return to work. The authorities, with the active cooperation of the Communist Party of France, re-asserted their control by bringing the weighty institutions of an advanced capitalist democracy to bear upon the masses. Let us return to the narrative and see how this occurred.

The movement reached its zenith near the end of May. From 27 May to 30 May the Gaullist government was in a visible political crisis, from which it seemed it might not survive. De Gaulle fled Paris on 29 May, to communicate with France's military commanders – leaving us in no doubt that the regime was quite prepared to use large-scale military force if it could not hold on to power by other means. But, as it turned out, "other means" triumphed.

Some observers thought that de Gaulle was at the point of resigning his office. But it was clear on

30 May that he personally was going to fight back. In the afternoon he gave a terse, defiant, speech on national television. The National Assembly would be immediately dissolved, and general elections held. He announced the formation of civic action squads to "defend the republic", and hinted at the use of force if things did not go his way.

From then on the movement was in retreat. A few strikes in the weaker sectors were broken in the next few days. A patchy back-to-work movement began. The Communist Party and its trade union federation, the CGT, was completely thrown off balance. Their shaky response to the calling of the elections and de Gaulle's defiance was to offer to talk to the government about wages and conditions. The Communist and Socialist Party agreed to participate in the elections. But they went farther than that; they staked everything on the electoral outcome. They, with their bureaucratic and reformist outlook, saw no further purpose for the mass strikes – they were seen as a possible embarrassment to their electoral support. In contrast, the student movement, and the various Trotskyist and other far-left organisations, saw no need to meet the Gaullist challenge in the electoral field. They urged a continuation of the mass strikes and declared that the outcome of the revolt would be determined in the factories and on the streets. Some groups even made calls for a rather undefined "workers' government". Others cried "all power to the soviets". Unfortunately, soviets did not exist as a generalised institution in 1968. A parliament did.

The Communist daily paper *l'Humanité* urged

and cajoled the workers to go back to work. It, along with the bourgeois press, exaggerated the extent of the patchy return-to-work in an attempt to create an anti-strike bandwagon. Its political message was this: why carry on with an exhausting and unrewarding strike when we can change things at the polls? Having no apparent alternative the workers drifted slowly back to work, helped by the promise of a fattened wage packet, or by threat of force by the riot police. A state of 'dual power" did not exist in May-June 1968. There were no widespread workers' councils. On the whole the workers were firmly under the leadership of the Communist Party, and that party was actively sabotaging the mass strikes. There seemed to be no alternative to the electoral struggle.

On June 12 most of the far-left organisations were banned. By the second week in June the back-to-work bandwagon really was rolling, with widespread effect. Riot police were used to smash pockets of resistance, leading to the deaths of some workers. On the day of the first round of the elections, 23 June, the greatest mass striked in history had ended. As Seale and McConville put it: "a classic parliamentary election came to put an end to a crisis which was, in essence, extra-parliamentary". *(French Revolution 1968,* p.125).

In the first round of the elections both the Communist and the Socialist parties each lost about two per cent of their previous vote. The only party which had supported the student struggles and mass strikes, whilst seeing the need to intervene at the electoral level as well, was the small *Partie*

*Socialiste Unifié*. It increased its poll from about two to four per cent. The Gaullists won the election with an increased vote of six per cent. Their victory was consolidated in the second round, on 30 June. De Gaulle was firmly back in power and the French revolt had ended.

### *The Significance of the Elections*

Despite the use of force by the Gaullist state, the killing and injury of several people and the forceful evacuation of some occupied factories, force does not suffice as an explanation of the end of the strike of ten million workers. The main reasons why the strike was ended are to do with the fact that France had a weighty tradition of parliamentary democracy. The French proletariat saw the electoral field as the only legitimate place where such a massive contest could be resolved. To some, this may be regrettable. But it was a fact, and theory and strategy have to take account of such facts. Second, the mass strike did not, regrettably, throw up widespread organs of workers' democracy. To a democratic Communist or Socialist in May 1968 there were no alternative institutions which could prefigure a democratic and socialist future. Third, the calling of the election made it relatively easy for the Communist Party to divert the strikes into purely economic struggles. Their more widespread political dimension was lost. It should be clear that parliamentary institutions in France are not a mere facade, and they act as a powerful force, for good or ill.

What should the revolutionary left have done

after the announcement of the elections on May 30? In order to maintain the confidence and combativity of the workers it was necessary to agitate for the continuation of the mass strikes. In order to stabilise and defend the strikes, to prevent police attacks and any back-to-work bandwagon, it was necessary to agitate for geographically-based workers' and students' councils. These things were in fact done, with some small but notable successes. But, on the whole, after that the revolutionary left went wrong. It argued that the elections were irrelevant. This allowed the Gaullists to characterise the revolutionaries as having no respect for existing democratic institutions: as being "dictators" and "totalitarians". Some sections of the revolutionary left, in adventurist fashion, needlessly promoted some riots after May 30. Unlike the previous struggles in May, which had the clear purpose of defending the students from repression and police attack, the June riots did not help matters. The relationship of forces had changed and a measure of retreat was necessary in the Latin Quarter. Finally, the entire revolutionary left outside the PSU argued for a boycott of the general elections. Not only did this reinforce the Gaullist caricature of the revolutionaries as anti-democratic, but it aided the defeat of the May 1968 movement in French society as a whole. In the minds of the majority of the French people the defeat of the Communist and Socialist Parties at the polls was a signal that the mass social movement of May and June 1968 no longer was within the bounds of political *legitimacy*. Every social system generates, *within itself,* a set of criteria which demarcate legitimate from illegitimate social practices. Marxists and others may object to the particular demarcation in a specific society, but it still has to be recognised that the process of legitimation does go on, and we should never confuse the actual situation with that which we, ourselves, might find most desirable. In an advanced capitalist parliamentary democracy such as France the electoral process and its outcome is a major component of the process of legitimation. To the majority of the French working class, the defeat of the left at the polls meant that any continuance of a mass extra-parliamentary struggle would have had no legitimacy. On the other hand, if the combined Communist, Socialist and PSU vote had been greater than that of the right then that would have been a clear signal for the mass struggle to go on.

Some may argue, in response, that it was necessary to 'smash parliamentary illusions"; so the boycott of the elections by the far left was correct on those grounds. Such a position would be unrealistic, unfounded and utopian. It would take no account of the relationship of forces between the far left and the rest of the working class. It would take no account of the weight and significance of parliamentary institutions in French society. It would take no account of the processes of legitimation. It is true that parliaments, as they exist in most capitalist societies, do have severe limitations, and most people do have illusions about them. But this situation is not altered by sitting on the sidelines, outside the electoral process. Illusions are not dispelled by presenting people with slogans. Illusions are dispelled in the very practice of struggle and *utilisation* of existing institutions. It is true that parliament has to be supplemented by other mass democratic institutions. But the limitations of parliamentary democracy can only be demonstrated in the process of working through it. This means that the far left should not only have participated in the elections but also it should have dropped its advocacy of the "smashing" of parliamentary institutions.

More than that – the French far left should have had a *electoral strategy* in June 1968. It should have worked to build up the PSU vote in the first round of the elections. As it happened, althought the PSU did increase its vote, a large number of students and other voters abstained in the elections. It is strangely ironic that organisations such as the French Section of the Mandel-led Trotskyist Fourth International later saw the increase in the PSU vote as an indication of significant minority support for the May 1968 movement. This particular result is quoted with pride, but at the time the Trotskyist groups advocated a complete boycott of the elections and did little to help the PSU or any other party.

The PSU was in fact eliminated in the first round of the elections. The parties of the left together got 41 per cent of the vote and the Gaullists 44 per cent. It was unlikely that the far left could have stopped the elimination of the PSU but it could have increased the aggregate vote of the left. Given the elimination of the PSU in the first round the problem was what to do in the second round, when all the small parties had been eliminated, and the electorate faced, in the main, a choice between the Communists, the Socialists and the Gaullists. This could have been forseen, and that meant, as soon as the election was announced on May 30, the left should have campaigned for an electoral alliance, in particular between the Socialists and Communists. As it happened De Gaulle managed to drive a wedge between these two major parties. Given that situation the left should have probably voted for the Communist Party, despite its sabotaging role, and its chequered and Stalinist political record. (The political record of Labour Governments in Britain is no less chequered, but it is still correct to campaign for the Labour Party in elections.) The attainment of an increased Communist vote in France would have probably done most to develop the mass struggle.

The experience of May 1968 in France does not show that a purely insurrectionary road to socialism is possible. Neither does it validate a purely electoralist perspective. The real lesson of May 1968 is this; both mass struggle and socialist electoral advance are necessary for the socialist transformation, and progress on one of these two fronts conditions and reinforces progress on the other. The socialist transformation will be achieved by a dialectic of mass struggle and electoral advance. May 1968 points to *that* future pattern of transformation, not to the scenario of Russia 1917.

We could illustrate this interaction between mass struggle and electoral advance with a number of examples. We could discuss the election of the Roosevelt administration in the 1930s in the United States, with its New Deal legislation and legitimation of trade union activity, leading to important mass struggles. We could discuss the miners' strike in Britain in 1974 and its interaction with electoral events, leading to the victory of the Labour Party in the general election and to certain key advances on the trade union front in the first few months of the Labour Government. We could discuss events in Chile and Portugal. However, it is far beyond the scope of this work to deal with these events in an adequate manner. We shall return to our general discussion of strategic imperatives for advanced capitalist democracies.

### *The Electoral Legitimation of Socialist Advance*

We have already discussed the process of legitimation in brief, in the context of May and June 1968. The fullest discussion of that process within capitalism is in Miliband's *The State and Capitalist Society.* Unfortunately, in that work, Miliband does not give much attention to the way in which the socialist left can *use* the process of legitimation for socialist ends. However, in a later article on the coup in Chile *(Socialist Register 1973)* he lays down a number of important strategic guidelines. Whilst making it clear that it was necessary for the Allende socialist government to build up a network of mass democratic institutions at the grass-roots, and that Allende largely failed in that task, he argues that this could not have been done independently of the parliamentary arena nor without parliamentary legitimation. This is an important insight, which puts a different perspective on the events in Chile. It contrasts with both the position of the far-left and of reformist social-democracy. The former argued that the parliamentary road was *necessarily* doomed to failure, the latter argued that it was the *only* place where reform could be enacted. Miliband's position, in short, advances a third road to socialism: a *dual perspective* of parliamentary and extra-parliamentary struggle.

Even with governments far less radical than the Allende regime in Chile the advantages of this dual perspective can be perceived. The Labour Government's repeal of the Tory Industrial Relations Act in 1974, and subsequent legislation in industry, has placed the trade unions at a higher level of influence, which, despite the setback in living standards since 1975, will be a significant factor in, for example, struggles against a future Tory Government. The discussion subsequent to the publication of the Bullock Report on Industrial Democracy in 1977, despite the severe inadequacies of that document, has placed the questions of worker participation and worker control firmly on the agenda.

In Britain there are some highly interesting examples of the dialectic of parliamentary and extra-parliamentary action in the non-industrial sphere. In the 1960s there was an unofficial and uncoordinated movement of activists into the working-class communities of the large cities. These activists were largely libertarian in their political outlook and had taken up unpaid community work after the decline of the Campaign for

Nuclear Disarmament and the onset of disillusionment with the post-1964 Labour Government. Eventually, after 1968, both national and local government, for various reasons, gave these community workers official status and allocated funds to community work. There are dangers and limits to this official legitimation of community work. But there are positive aspects to it as well. The extent and effectiveness of community work has been increased, and it has reached the stage where the community worker is playing a not insignificant role in the raising of the political consciousness of certain sections of the working class.

A second example from Britain is the rise of the Women's Liberation Movement after 1969. This movement spread, both inside and outside industry, to remarkable dimensions, in a short space of time. It fuelled a struggle for equal pay for women, and set up a network of discussion groups for employed women and housewives. Eventually this grass-roots movement gave rise to a response from the Tory Government, which introduced an inadequate bill on equal pay. This legislation was improved and extended, but not sufficiently, under the subsequent Labour administration. The effect of this raising of the issue at the parliamentary level, however, has been very significant. First it has become an important issue within party politics and, more crucially, the Labour Party and the established institutions of the labour movement. Second, it has led to an extended public discussion of the issue of women's equality, and an evaluation of the question in most spheres of private and public life. These advances could not have been made by the Women's Liberation Movement without the intrusion of the issue into the parliamentary arena. Furthermore, the existence of legislation for equal pay on the statute books, inadequate as it is, has led to a series of strikes for the enforcement of the principle and spirit of those Acts.

Given the non-radical nature of all Labour Governments up to now, such advances, despite their limited nature, are indicative of greater possibilities under a socialist government really bent on social change. All past Labour Governments have not attempted such a transformation, and have spent their time simply patching up and managing capitalism. However, the Labour *Party*, during its period of radicalisation (in the constituences and affiliated trade unions) after 1970, has produced a number of useful ideas which a future socialist government could utilise to start the process of transformation and involve the working class in socialist change. One of the most important of these is the Planning Agreement, which synthesises the struggle for workers' control at the level of the enterprise with the struggle for a planned economy. The Labour Government's Industry Bill, enacted in 1975, contained Planning Agreements in a much watered-down and mutilated form. The fact that the Planning Agreement idea has been very partially embodied in a piece of legislation means that it is quite possible and realistic to expect that they could play a major part in a future socialist strategy. As David Purdy put in a review of a book by Stuart Holland, the main originator of the Planning Agreement idea:

> There will those on the left who dismiss Holland's approach to policy as a reformist prop to capitalism. In my view this would be a serious misestimate. The planning agreements framework offers a rich solution to the old problem of how to link the long-term objective of socialism with the immediate conduct of class struggles. It provides a method of inscribing an alien, socialist logic into the workings of capitalism, and of generating self-activity amongst diverse social groups around programmes which embody the concrete, living meaning of socialism. In short, this approach to policy comes to terms with the requirements of a revolutionary strategy in the advanced bourgeois hegemony and the ruling capitalist power bloc. *(Capital and Class,* Spring 1977).

We can add to that, in the context of the theme of this work. The Planning Agreement strategy allows a powerful and effective interaction of struggle at the parliamentary and shop-floor levels. It is an example of a *dual strategy* for transforming the capitalist economy.

## *Are Reforms Impossible Under Capitalism?*

Some have argued that such a dual strategy is doomed because significant economic reforms are impossible under capitalism. The seizure of state power is necessary, by the working class, before any such economic transformation can be commenced. Some further argue that short of such a seizure of power, i.e. under the present capitalist system, any capitalist economic recovery must be accompanied by a smashing of the organisations of the working class and a reduction of living standards. Let us briefly deal with each of these three points in turn.

First, there is no adequate theoretical reason to deny the possibility of economic reforms. Furthermore, such a denial would fly in the face of the evidence of major advances in working class living standards in the last 100 years. Some Marxists seem to argue that *any* government within a capitalist system is forced to follow a single and inexorable path to serve the interests of capital. This view neglects both the relative autonomy of the state and the nature of capitalism for the last century, more especially in the post Second World War phase of capitalist development. If capitalism was ever perfectly competitive it is no longer so. Overwhelming competitive forces do not bear upon every firm, forcing it to fix prices, wages and the level of output within narrow margins. In most industries only a few firms are dominant. According to the economic theory of such an oligopolistic economy, prices, wages and levels of output are not determined; at least by purely economic forces alone. They can conceivably oscillate within wide margins. There is no rigid "law of value" (a term used but never explained in orthodox Marxist literature) or "hidden hand" forcing economic variables along a determined path. So in the real capitalist world it is quite possible that a whole series of economic variables can be altered by social and political forces. This does not mean that the ills of capitalism can be abolished simply by working class pressure. But it does mean that the working class can make some significant changes in economic circumstances, just as, for example, the British working class has managed to raise the level of its share of pre-tax national income in the last 20 years. Significant reforms are, therefore, possible, even within the framework of capitalist social relations, even within the immutable contradictions of capitalism.

Second, despite the fact that the capitalist system is facing a severe crisis there is no reason to assume that its way out of that crisis must, *necessarily*, involve the massive repression of the working class. In general the problem for capitalism is not simply one of increasing the share of profits in the national income, nor a question of simply shackling the trade unions. The problem for capitalism when it faces a period of stagnation or crisis at the economic level is one of *restructuring* the economy to obtain a greater pace of capital accumulation. This does not necessarily involve a cutting of living standards nor a repression of the working class. It could, for example, be achieved by increasing the productivity of industry, or by changing the structure of financial or industrial capital.

Consider the example of the 1930s. In that decade, despite a severe slump, trade union organisation grew by leaps and bounds in the United States. Living standards for the *employed* working class also rose to a significant degree. Although the extent of unemployment was a massive burden on the working class as a whole, it was not crucial in promoting a capitalist economic recovery. The recovery came about for several reasons, such as the tentative introduction of "New Deal" measures of economic stimulation, the concentration of capital into fewer and fewer large firms, and the growth of the consumer durables industry. There is no historical or theoretical evidence to indicate that capitalism necessarily requires a massive repression of the working class to recover from a severe crisis. Although, it must be admitted, that certainly does not include the *possibility* of such repression.

Third, the idea that the seizure of power by the working class must precede any socialist economic transformation may have been appropriate to Russia in 1917 but it is not applicable to advanced capitalist democracies. It is inapplicable because it is unrealistic and theoretically unfounded. It assumes that a socialist revolutionary consciousness must be generated within a majority of the working class before any concrete socialist change is effective. This consciousness is seen to spring from the reflex actions of the working class in circumstances of capitalist exploitation and repression, or from the dispensing of revolutionary ideas amongst the masses, or from the leadership and organisation provided by a revolutionary party, or from a combination of all three. This crude theory of the generation of a revolutionary consciousness ignores two crucial facets of modern capitalist reality. The role of *institutions* in the formation of political consciousness is ignored: institutions such as parliament and the established organisations of the working class. The relationship of forces between the revolutionary and non-revolutionary left is ignored, and it is assumed that revolutionary consciousness will grow simply as a result of the dedication and will of a small minority. A realistic theory of the generation of revolutionary socialist consciousness must take account of the fact that consciousness is largely generated and refracted by institutions, and by the practicalities of the situation determined by the *relationship of political forces* in and out of parliament.

### *The Raising of Working-Class Consciousness*

The traditional Leninist and Trotskyist attitude to parliament under capitalism is to use it simply as a loudspeaker for socialist propaganda. Elections are contested for propaganda reasons, and votes are necessary only insofar as to elect a revolutionary member of parliament who can then place his mouth at the sharp end of the loudspeaker. Only a few Members of Parliament are necessary for this task, for the real struggle is seen to go on outside. It is in the extra-parliamentary arena that the orthodox Trotskyist programme of "transitional demands" comes to the fore. The transitional demand, not parliament, is seen as the major element in raising working class consciousness.

The notion of a transitional demand has had varied and often ambiguous applications to Trotskyist practice. Crudely, it was summed up by Trotsky as follows:

> Not one of our demands will be realised under capitalism. That is why we are calling them transitional demands. It creates a bridge to the mentality of the workers and then a material bridge to the socialist revolution. (*Writings*, 1938-9, p.44)

The idea is that in struggling for an unrealisable demand within the capitalist system, such as the "sliding scale" or indexation of wages to prices, the masses will be mobilized into ever more intensive struggle. Eventually, through the agency of the revolutionary party, the struggle will reach revolutionary proportions.

First we can note, as a relatively minor point, that several of the demands in the Trotskyist *Transitional Programme* have in fact been met under capitalism. For instance, in some countries, such as Belgium, a sliding scale of wages has existed for decades. In Britain some legal provision has been made to allow the trade unions to inspect business records: another "transitional demand". A demand to "state-ize the credit system" has been largely realised in France where the state has control of 85 per cent of all bank deposits. Several of the demands in the *Transitional Programme* are not so unrealizable, even under capitalism.

The real point of criticism of the *Transitional Programme* is that it embodied a false notion of the development of revolutionary socialist consciousness. First it assumes that a mere idea, a transitional demand, will be taken up by the masses in the appropriate situation simply because a revolutionary group is expounding that idea. Although there are rare examples of such a thing happening, the flight of the idea from programme to masses does not often take place. The transitional demand formula ignores the fact that most often it is not *what* is said that matters, but *who* says it. Hence the flight of an idea is guided by the type of *institution* that is expounding that idea and the *relationship of forces* between the expounding institution and the masses, and in society at large. Many many Trotskyist groups have been advocating workers' occupations and workers' control for many years, with very rare success. Yet a leading figure in the Labour Party, Tony Benn, got the idea across of an occupation of Upper Clyde Shipbuilders which was taken up by the workers in a major and famous struggle. Also it was Tony Benn who suggested the idea of a plan for socially useful production to the Lucas Aerospace shop stewards. This again became a major landmark of working class struggle, when those shop stewards waged the campaign for their "corporate plan". It is figures such as Benn, "warts and all", who can have a far greater effect on working class struggle and consciousness than the loud and frequent pronouncements of the many Trotskyist groups. This efficacy is not mainly due to the personality or subjective power of such a person, but to his position in the leading institutions of the labour movement. Turning away from single personalities, there are many examples of the influence of a major institution of the labour movement, such as the Labour Party itself, on the course of future struggle. The idea of a 'Council of Action" as a form of proto-soviet, is often advanced by the far left in Britain. This is a direct reference to the actual Councils of Action which were set up in various localities in the General Strike of 1926. But these Councils of Action were not formed spontaneously; the idea for their formation in 1926 did not come from the heads of a few inspired individuals. Actually the first Councils of Action were formed in 1920 by local Labour Parties and Trades Councils in response to the national initiative of the Labour Party to organise against British imperialist intervention in the Russian Civil War. The idea of a Council of Action only gained widespread acceptance because of the initial role of the Labour Party in publicising it.

Second, the *Transitional Programme* assumes that on the event of a group of workers accepting the need to implement one of its demands they will necessarily be motivated to act in pursuit of that demand, even if we admit that the role of a revolutionary nucleus is crucial in this respect. Given the nature of those demands, which are said by that revolutionary nucleus to be unrealisable under capitalism, the masses are more likely to relapse into apathy or despair, rather than to take on the capitalist system all in one go. The mere acceptance of the desirability of a demand is not sufficient. Both the means of achieving it have to be at hand, and the goal itself has to be realistic, otherwise people will not risk life and limb in active struggle. This is not to say that the masses are not capable of struggling fervently, for noble and revolutionary proportions in *defence* of an existing gain, such as the defence of the Popular Front government at the start of the Spanish Civil War in 1936. Even the Bolshevik revolution was mobilised around slogans for the defence of the existing Soviets against the threat of a right-wing reaction. In short, therefore, the masses are not mobilised simply because the appropriate idea enters their heads. They are moved to action, even revolutionary action, only when the task they face is apparently realistic and the practical means for its implementation actually exist.

In short, the main fault of the *Transitional Programme* stems from what may be termed its *ideologism.* By that we mean that ideas and ideology are seen as the main spurs to mass action. Once again, the key role of *institutions* and the *relationship of forces* is neglected. This ideologism accounts for much of the sectarianism and hair-splitting of most of the Trotskyist groups, because for them the main issue is to "present correct ideas". Organisational weight and credibility are sacrificed for pristine ideological purity, even at the cost of many splits and expulsions.

It may appear that we have deviated from the main topic under discussion: parliamentary democracy. But in fact the course of our argument now leads us straight back to that theme. We have argued above that reforms are possible under modern capitalism. We have also emphasised the role of institutions in social and revolutionary change. Given those arguments we can now pose a strategy, in outline, that will provide a feasible basis for socialist change in advanced capitalist democracies.

## *A Transitional Political and Economic Programme*

Socialist change will not come about merely by presenting an idea, such as a transitional demand, to the masses. It is also necessary to show the means and possibility of socialism. The first step that a socialist party must thus achieve is to demonstrate its ability to gain the support, expressed in the conventional way, of the majority of the electorate.

That means, of course, gaining a majority in parliament. That step does not in itself signify that the means of socialist change are available but that socialism has been legitimated by the electoral process, and that the socialist movement is thus strengthened.

Once a socialist party is in power it has the chance, through its political and economic programme, to demonstrate and involve people in the practical possibility of socialism. This will involve such measures as calling upon people to organise popular institutions of power at the grass-roots level; the role of parliament will be to *strengthen* these institutions by giving them legal endorsement. At the economic level the socialist government will orchestrate a programme of economic transformation involving both the formal nationalisation of the major firms in the economy and the encouragement and support an extension of workers' control at every stage of economic management. As we have stated above, parliament on its own cannot accomplish the complete political and economic transformation. Also the parliamentary struggle is often likely to be a *delayed* reflection of previous mass struggles. However, that does not mean that the parliamentary struggle can be ignored, neither can the task of achieving a majority of elected socialists in parliament.

The full transitional political and economic programme will have to be worked out after concrete investigation into national and local conditions. Such a programme would differ from the ideologistic *Transitional Programme* of the Trotskyists in that it would not simply rely on the force of ideas emanating from a small revolutionary nucleus. It would be a programme with institutional and material grounding. It would not simply contain a promise of a seemingly far off socialist milleniun, but be capable of partial realisation within the bounds of capitalist reality. It would not be a dogmatic and unverified proscription for activity, according to formulae which have never succeeded in advanced capitalist democracies, but a programme that would be capable of modification in the light of practical achievement. In short, it would be wedded to the *practical process* of socialist change rather than the mere *ideas* and earnest wishes of groups with little central implanation in the socialist movement.

It must be made clear, however, that the socialist programme must recognise and advocate preparations for possible resistance by reactionary armed forces. Neither must such a programme assume that the process of socialist transformation can go on in a gradualistic fashion. At one stage or another the socialist transformation is likely to involve a decisive political contest, ending, hopefully, in the complete transfer of economic and political power to the working majority of the population. That contest could take a variety of forms. It need not involve violence or civil war, but if the reactionary forces present this sort of threat then it must be met with force. The socialist movement must not make the same mistake as in Chile: either to ignore or rely on the "goodwill" of the army. Socialism will not be secure until the threat of reactionary force is removed.

### *The Military Balance of Forces*

It is worth emphasising that the foundation of any political system is the physical force of the state. In times of social peace and concord the forces of law, argument and moral persuasion have a major and pronounced role. But times of social conflict and crisis can strip away the veneers of normalcy and reveal the rough might of the armed forces. Mere words are no match for bombs and bullets.

Such arguments are often *counterposed* to a strategy which involves obtaining a majority in parliament. In fact, in advanced capitalist democracies, military considerations *require* that the socialist movement attains that electoral goal. This statement can be supported with a simple but forceful argument, based on the following axioms. First, the ability of reactionary military forces to repress or overturn a mass socialist movement is inversely proportional, other things being equal, to the mass support that socialist movement enjoys. Furthermore, the success of a reactionary military offensive will depend, to some extent, on the degree of active support it can call upon in the civilian population. For example, civilians can be used by the army to spy on socialists, relay information, and break strikes. There is also the possibility that fascist squads would be formed from violently anti-socialist civilians, as in Italy and Germany in the inter-war years. In short, a reactionary army will have more difficulty in mounting anti-socialist repression if the socialist movement has vast mass support, as all "counter-insurgency" operations are affected considerably by the degree of support or opposition amongst the civilian population.

Second, given the weight of parliamentary institutions in advanced capitalist democracies, mass support for the socialist movement will be greater if that movement has achieved a majority in parliament. Third, the active anti-socialist sector of the civilian population will be smaller, or less able to function, if a socialist parliamentary majority is in existence. These two axioms are based on our previous theoretical analysis of parliamentary legitimation, and can find historical support in the experiences of Germany 1918-19, France 1968, and Chile 1970-73.

It is clear from these three axioms that the military relationship of forces depends, to a considerable extent, on the electoral success of the socialist movement. Let us compare two hypothetical situations in an advanced capitalist democracy. The first is a situation where a mass socialist movement has dissolved the traditional parliament and replaced it by a national congress of soviets. The second is a situation where a national network of soviets exists alongside the existing parliament, within which a socialist government has an elected majority, and has provided legal endorsement of soviets. There is little doubt that in a country such as Britain the army would have a much greater chance of overturning a socialist regime in the first case, rather than the second. In the second case the military balance of forces will be more favourable to the working class and their allies. This does not mean, of course, that a socialist parliamentary majority would *ensure* military victory: such a view would be absurd. We simply state that a socialist parliamentary majority *aids* the socialist military struggle. In a country with a weighty tradition of parliamentary democracy there will be many people, both socialists and non-socialists, who will be prepared to defend an elected socialist government against a reactionary coup. Furthermore, a *non-socialist* parliamentary majority could be used to legitimate the use of reactionary force against the socialist movement. Whereas the existence of a socialist majority in parliament will *prevent* reactionary forces from using that institution as a rubber stamp for reaction. Just as ideas, as Marx pointed out, become a material force when they grip the minds of the masses, so do institutions. such as parliament, become material forces in a military showdown: they can be used on one side or the other, and they are unlikely to retire from the scene in benevolent neutrality. To vacate parliament, to leave it with a non-socialist majority, are ways of providing the forces of reaction with valuable ammunition for the forcible suppression of socialism. Although the existence of a parliamentary majority does not, of course, ensure victory for either side

We have now provided arguments to support propositions 9 and 10. We now turn to propositions 11 and 12, which involve a discussion of soviets.

## *Soviets and Parliament*

The soviet, a council of workers, soldiers and peasants elected from the workplaces and barracks in a particular locality, first emerged in the Russian revolution of 1905. The strategies of the far left usually pose soviets as an alternative to parliamentary democracy: *either* soviets *or* parliament. The former is "proletarian democracy" the latter is "bourgeois democracy". However, it is not so well known that even in an autocratic country such as Russia, with a miniscule tradition of parliamentary democracy, the masses saw parliamentary reform as one of the main goals, and the soviets were partly set up to pursue that aim. In 1905 the workers from the St. Petersburg Soviet first advanced the following main demand:

> We proclaim a political strike and will fight to the last for the summoning of a Constituent Assembly on the basis of universal, equal, direct and secret suffrage to introduce a democratic republic in Russia. (Source: L. Trotsky, *1905*, Pelican, p. 124.).

Later, of course, during 1917 under Bolshevik influence the soviets aspired to exclusive power. Although the Bolsheviks may have had no alternative to abolishing the Constituent Assembly after the October Revolution, it is important to realise that even in an autocracy such as Russia parliamentary forms did have considerable ideological and social weight.

In Western Europe the social weight of parliamentary institutions is so great that the Bolshevik strategy, appropriate for conditions in Russia in 1917, is rendered inapplicable. This does not deny the necessity of the formation of institutions of mass popular power, such as soviets. However, soviets are likely to have an organic and indissoluble link with parliament, given the significance of the latter in moulding political action. As Ken Coates has put it:

> No magic barricades will sweep it all away and inaugurate a promised utopia, no soviets will reemerge in pristine order from the textbooks, and no self-appointed elects will impose their rigorous orthodoxies on stevedores and coalminers, or even teachers and computer-programmers, simply because the politicians have failed again. The soviets, which might be desirable, to say nothing of the orthodoxies, which certainly would not, *could* arrive at hegemony: but only in defence of gains already made within the given constitutional order. *(Socialists and the Labour Party,* p. 21.).

And again in the same work:

> Short of a "cold" counter-revolution, if soviets were ever to emerge in Britain, it would be in defence of the right of Parliament to assert its alleged prerogatives, rather than as abstractly desirable bodies. (p. 24n).

There is rich historical evidence to support Coates' conjecture that soviets, if formed, would have a *defensive* aim. Even the most radical and sweeping of revolutions are triggered, not because someone hangs an abstract ideal before the eyes of the masses, but because the progress of events often impels the masses into actions which, although conceived as defensive, have the objective effect of a revolutionary offensive. Even a revolution on the purely insurrectionary model is less likely to succeed without such a defensive formulation. The Bolsheviks, including Trotsky, were well aware of this. As Trotsky put in in his *History of the Russian Revolution:*

Although an insurrection can win on the offensive, it develops better, the more it looks like self-defence. (Sphere Books edition, vol. 3, p. 195).

For that reason the Bolsheviks used the obstructions and provocations of the Provisional Government as a "legal" pretext for the "defensive" act of the insurrection, which was conceived as necessary to protect the soviets from threat of repression. It is significant that even in an autocratic country such as Russia the appeal to legality was regarded as important. Trotsky again:

The attacking side is almost always interested in seeming on the defensive. A revolutionary party is interested in legal coverings. (Ibid., p. 259).

These guidelines, when applied to advanced capitalist democracies, must assume an even greater significance. James P. Cannon, a veteran Trotskyist, wrote:

defensive formulations are an indispensable medium for teaching the masses, who will not be convinced by theory but only by their own experience and propaganda related thereto. This experience of the masses proceeds in the main along the line of defensive actions. That is why defensive formulations are most easily comprehensible and represent the best approach of the revolutionary Marxists to the masses. Finally, it is a tactical and legal consideration of no small importance in a bourgeois democratic country that defensive formulas partially disarm the class enemy; or in any case, make their attacks more difficult and costly. Why should such advantages be thrown away? *(What Policy for Revolutionists – Marxism or Ultra-Leftism?*, p. 59).

It appears that many modern Trotskyists have much

to learn from Trotsky and Cannon! However, what these two revolutionaries do not emphasis in their writings is that the efficacy of the defensive formulation is not due to its abstract defensiveness, but because it is a call to defend an *existing gain or institution* which is seen in a positive light by the masses. Hence the defensive formulation of the call to mobilise for insurrection in 1917 was posed in terms of defence of soviet power.

Cannon rightly points out that defensive formulations are "of no small importance" when applied to advanced capitalist democracies. But what are the relevant gains or institutions in such countries? They must include the various reforms that have been instituted, pertaining to trade union rights, for example, and democratic institutions such as parliament. It is highly unlikely, therefore, that a revolutionary movement would succeed in such countries if it gave itself the non-defensive aim of smashing or violating parliament. It may be argued in response that the role of soviets may well be to *defend* themselves and the working class movement against repression enacted by a reactionary parliament. No doubt such circumstances are possible, even probable. But the point is that such a conjuncture is unlikely to develop into a socialist transformation; given the weight of parliamentary institutions it is likely to *remain* defensive. Only a defensive struggle which can call upon parliament as an ally and legitimator of its actions is likely to develop into a successful offensive on the capitalist order.

### *Should Parliament be Subordinated to the Soviets?*

Assuming that a network of soviets, or something similar, did emerge in a country such as Britain, should they aspire to supremacy over the existing parliament after the socialist revolution? Many of our arguments above support the view that they should not. Further arguments can be brought forward to support the same conclusion. The most important of which is that the soviet, whilst being an excellent body for mass action and agitation, has limitations as a universal representative body. We do not refer to the principle of direct recall of delegates; that principle could and should be applied to parliament. We refer to the capacity of the soviet to claim the allegiance of all sectors of the working population.

The first sector of the population that a soviet would represent inadequately would be housewives. It may be possible for a body of housewives to elect delegates, under recall of course, to the local soviet. But this sector would still be at a disadvantage in comparison to groups of workers in large factories, for the reason that housewives would not be united daily in a single institution, and would have only limited access to their elected soviet delegate. They would be less able than the workers in the factories to monitor the actions of their delegate, and less informed by regular common discussion with others in the same social group. This is not to say that parliamentary representation is without its defects. But it is clear that soviet representation, despite its advantages, does perpetuate the inferior social and political status of housebound women.

The second sector that concerns us is the self-employed. In most capitalist countries they constitute about one-tenth of the working population, and show no sign of disappearing, even in the face of the progressive concentration and internationalisation of capital. Their social and cultural influence extends beyond that. Many workers have the ambition to become self-employed, as a means of apparently evading the direct and daily despotism of capitalistic management. This means that the fortunes of the self-employed are loosely related to the aspirations of many workers, even if many of these workers have little chance of actually becoming self-employed. It is necessary for a socialist movement to attempt to win over the self-employed to the socialist cause, by assuring them that their rights and self-employment status would remain under socialism; it would disappear only if they *voluntarily* entered the ranks of the proletariat. Given this necessity of a class alliance with the self-employed the desirability of the *supremacy* of a soviet-style organisation is again placed in doubt. For similar reasons to housewives, soviet organisation would grossly discriminate against the self-employed. This is not an argument against soviets, as the industrial proletariat must remain the main vehicle for social change; and activist, soviet-style organisations must reflect this. It is an argument for the supremacy of a parliamentary form of representation which can claim and receive the allegiance of *all* layers of the working population. Mass institutions, such as soviets, are an indispensable organ for socialist change, for enforcing and preserving workers' power. But they need to be complemented by parliamentary organisation in order to hegemonise the traditionally politically backward sections of this society, such as house-bound women and the self-employed.

More generally, there is a danger that factory-based soviet-style organisation could sustain a parochial and particularistic consciousness among workers, just as contemporary trade unionism often sustains a defensive and non-hegemonic attitude. The interests of the workers in a particular factory or locality would dwarf the general interests of the working masses as a whole. Again this is not an argument for abolishing soviets; it is an argument for *synthesising* them with the parliamentary form of representation. Parliament would act as a counter-balance, an expression of the general interest in counterposition to particular will of the soviet. It would be the main arena for bringing together the various aspirations of the workers, for the forging of a common hegemonic policy.

### *Should Capitalists Have the Vote?*

It might be argued that traditional parliamentary representation would give the capitalist class the vote, and that they should not receive such a privilege. Although we may agree that such a vote is not deserved, there are good political reasons for implementing universal adult suffrage. First, in advanced capitalist countries today capitalists constitute less than five per cent of the adult population, and their vote is likely to make little difference. Second, the granting of the vote to the capitalists, under the banner of universal suffrage, will prevent the reactionaries using its absence as a rallying cry for the overthrow of the socialist regime. Once again it is a question of making the *legitimacy* of the socialist transformation visible to the entire world, of denying the right of reactionaries the claim to represent true and complete democracy. Under modern conditions, there is a negligible disadvantage, and much advantage, in maintaining the system of universal suffrage.

## *The "Dictatorship of the Proletariat"*

The term "dictatorship of the proletariat" has assumed the status of a major shibboleth in the Marxist movement. Marx and Engels used it occasionally, sometimes with undefined meaning. In one single statement, however, Marx gave adherence to that goal the status of supreme orthdoxy. Writing to Weydemeyer in 1852 he endorsed the historical necessity of the dictatorship of the proletariat, and suggested that it was the main and central feature of Marxist thought. In that letter, however, he was less forthright in describing what form that dictatorship would take. It was Engels who gave it historical substance, when he described the Paris Commune of 1871 as the dictatorship of the proletariat.

The term was used more frequently by Lenin, in works such as *The State and Revolution*:

> The dictatorship of the proletariat, the period of transition to communism, will for the first time create democracy for the people, for the majority, along with

> the necessary suppression of the exploiters, of the minority.

This "democracy for the people" was in the form of soviet power, of mass involvement in political decisions and actions. It was not equated with the dictatorship of an individual, party, or elite; it was the dictatorship of a *class*.

However, history gave Stalin the opportunity to endow the term "dictatorship of the proletariat" with his own distinctive meaning, quite different to that which was intended by Marx, Engels, or Lenin. Stalin's "dictatorship of the proletariat" was the dictatorship of *himself*, claiming to act on *behalf* of the proletariat. References to the texts of Marx, Engels and Lenin, were taken, twisted, and used to justify one of the most repressive regimes in history. The "dictatorship of the proletariat" was Stalin's slogan as he engineered the extermination of over five million peasants and the imprisonment and execution of hundreds of thousands of loyal Communists.

It is undeniable that the term has been indelibly stained with the blood of those millions that died under Stalin. Whatever democratic content the term might have had has been virtually extinguished. Despite the intentions of those that attempt to maintain the true spirit of the "dictatorship of the proletariat", as intimated in the works of Marx and Lenin, to the majority of the population the term means despotism, the denial of democracy, and the rule by an individual or elite. The abominations of the Soviet regime have extinguished the possibility of conveying the original meaning on a mass scale.

In any case it is extremely difficult to popularise the proposition that in the case of "the dictatorship of the proletariat" the word "dictatorship" really means democracy for the majority. It flies in the face of the accepted meaning of the word "dictatorship". And dictionary will define the word as "state ruled by a dictator", a state which "suppresses democratic government". Like it or not these are the accepted meanings of the word. Revolutionaries may be able to storm heaven and earth, but they will still have great difficulty in turning language upside down. If we define "two" as "the number of legs on a horse" then we can argue with validity that "two plus two equals eight". Unfortunately, most people will prefer to stick to the original meaning of the word "two", and be positively counter-revolutionary in such matters of language. And most people will show a great deal of bourgeois confusion when they are told that the "*dictatorship* of the proletariat" is the same thing as "proletarian *democracy*".

The fact is that the term "dictatorship of the proletariat" has become a *liability* for Marxism in advanced capitalist democracies. In popular imagination it shackles the movement to Stalin's despotism. Whatever it may have originally meant to Marx and Lenin the term itself should be abandoned. Of course it is necessary to point out that Marx and Lenin would have been horrified by Stalin's dictatorship, and that Lenin began to struggle against the degeneration of the Soviet regime in his later years. But the struggle was lost, and Marxism has to continue and reinforce a vigilant struggle against association with the abominations of Stalinism. In that process some ambiguous baggage has to be ditched. And were it not for that unfortunate letter of Marx to Weydemeyer of 1852 the term would have been ditched much earlier.

In abandoning the term "dictatorship of the proletariat" we do not wish to abandon the principle that the working classes should suppress the force, or threat of force, that may be employed by the capitalists. But we do not need the term "dictatorship" to enforce that point. Everyone is aware that even democratic regimes have employed force to resist the rebellion of a minority. The same principle will still apply to a socialist democracy. There should be little difficulty in explaining and justifying that: it is simply a matter of legitimate self-defence.

Our reasons for abandoning the term "dictatorship of the proletariat" are not the same as those advanced by the Communist Party of France, and the other Communist Parties which have since done the same thing. In the first case none of those Communist Parties have sufficiently extricated themselves from the trappings of Stalinism. In the past, when still used the term, it was never suggested that it *excluded* such a form of dictatorship that existed with Stalin. Furthermore, the truly Leninist idea of a network of democratic soviets representing the working masses at every level of management and government was an anathema to every Communist Party after 1930. Even today few Communist Parties advocate workers' control of production, or propose the formation of workers' councils to supplement existing democratic institutions. The rejection of the term "dictatorship of the proletariat" has, to them, meant the rejection of Stalinist dictatorship, and that is fortunate. But it has not been associated with the re-adoption of much that is valid in the Marxist-Leninist tradition since eclipsed by Stalinism. In the programmes of such parties we will find endless vague references to "advanced democracy", "extended democracy", "rule by the people" and so forth, but it is never spelt out what all this means. We search in vain for a clear statement that the transition to socialism must involve the creation of many directly representative democratic institutions at the grass roots level, each with their own powers and relative autonomy.

The Communist Parties of the Western World have a lot to do before they can completely and effectively disassociate themselves from the Stalinist heritage. If, like charity, democracy begins at home then it is clear that the task has hardly started, for in most parties inner party democracy is little more than a limited formality. Rejecting Stalinism means accepting not only the word but the spirit of the sort of democracy that has been advanced in the working class movement for over a century.

### *The Twin Millstones of Present-Day Marxism*

It is an unfortunate fact that post-war Marxism has been dominated by Stalinism, and that the only Marxist alternative of any viability has been a collection of Trotskyist and Maoist groups which have all set themselves the aim of smashing the entire state apparatus, including parliament, and posing the apparent confusion of a democratic proletarian dictatorship to replace all existing democratic institutions. As a result present-day Marxism has two millstones round its neck: both a muted Stalinism, found in the Communist Parties, and an unrealistic voluntarism of fundamentalist flavour, found in the groups of the far left. Yet Marxism, as a tradition, as a system of analysis, as a guide to the practice of creating a socialist society, still retains its vast riches. As yet there is no alternative science of modern society. But its future is not assured, unless the millstones are cast off. At the practical rather than the purely theoretical level a first priority is a re-assessment of parliamentary democracy.

Given the endemic conservatism of most of the Marxist organisations such an extension and revision of Marxist theory and practice will be resisted by many. The old false alternatives will pose the old lines of division: reform or revolution? Marxism or revisionism? Lenin or Kautsky? The old accusations will be repeated like an old record stuck in a weary groove. The high priests of orthodoxy will warn that the fundamentals of the faith are at stake.

We admit it. Orthodoxy may be at stake. But that is not all. The crisis of Marxist theory and practice is so deep that in addition the viability of Marxism as a developing science, and the socialist future itself, are also at stake. It may be difficult to accept, but orthodox Marxism, for many reasons, in particular its attitude to dictatorship and democracy, will not make much progress unless fundamental revisions are made. The choice, therefore, is not simply between orthodox Marxism and "revisionism", but between orthodox Marxism and a socialist future. At this juncture the dogmatic defence of rigid orthodoxy is a barrier to socialist advance. But fortunately the popularisation of Marxism in the 1960s and 1970s has produced much more than a proliferation of sects. It has created the possibility of a new and living Marxism which can apply the motto of Marx to Marxism itself:

"Merciless criticism of all things existing".

# A Reply to Shirley Williams

"no further progress can be made in seeking to get crumbs from the rich man's table . . . in the present condition of the world we are bound in duty to those whom we represent to tell them quite clearly that they cannot get socialism without tears, that whenever we try to do anything we will be opposed by every vested interest, financial, political and social, and I think we have got to face the fact, even if we are returned with a majority, we shall have to fight all the way . . . we have got to strike while the iron is hot".

Clement Attlee, Labour Party Conference, 1932

In December 1976 Tony Benn gave a forceful defence of the right of Marxists to remain in the Labour Party, and argued that Marxism had always been a significant influence on mainstream British socialism. The newspaper which carried his statement, *The Guardian,* was later, on 22 January 1977, to publish the text of a provocative speech by the Labour Minister of Education, Shirley Williams, which provided a rallying call for those who wished to see Trotskyists driven out of the Labour Party. The tone of the speech is virulent and uncomprimising. Its content is intelligently constructed; its design being to divide the entire left of the Party under the cover of an attack which appears to concentrate simply upon Trotskyism.

The title of the published text of her speech was *Trotskyism and Democracy*. In connecting these two issues she has touched on a weak spot in the Trotskyist and orthodox Leninist tradition. A weakness which I outlined in the previous essay; the underestimation of the weight of parliamentary democratic institutions, and the neglect of the task of obtaining parliamentary legitimation of the socialist transformation. Within the Leninist tradition Parliament is usually regarded as an empty facade, or at most a mere forum for socialist propaganda. This view is not only theoretically weak, it also leads to the type of attack cogently presented by Shirley Williams in her speech:

> To some Marxists, representative democracy – usually described as "bourgeois democracy" – is simply a sham. At a time when representative democracy and its associated civil liberties are far from safe, is it surprising that some of us distrust these half-hearted allies?

It is into this weak spot that Shirley Williams attempts to drive a wedge. It does not get very far. From astute observation she degenerates into factual distortion and political banality. In the process she herself reveals *her* weak links with the socialist tradition, and *her* rather limited advocacy of democracy in modern society.

## *Trotskyism, Communism and the Defence of Democracy*

On the basis of one or two unrepresentative

quotations from Marx and Trotsky it is alleged that there is little respect for democracy in the Marxist tradition. Trotsky, in particular, is said to hold "liberty and democracy in total contempt". Such a description is hardly compatible with the record of Trotsky's struggle against Stalinist totalitarianism in the Soviet Union, and his forceful opposition to Fascism in Europe. After the death of Lenin, Trotsky gave consistent opposition to the erosion of political freedom and civil liberties in the USSR, opposing the ban on factions within the Communist Party, advocating industrial democracy, and defending the democratic rights of national minorities. Despite the theoretical weaknesses in his appraisal of parliamentary democracy the charge of holding "liberty and democracy in total contempt" does not stand up to examination. Trotsky spent his life struggling against autocracy and totalitarianism; first against Tsarism then against Fascism and Stalinist dictatorship. Credit should be given where great credit is due.

The matter goes further than that. If we were to believe Shirley Williams, Marxists have been reluctant tail-enders in the struggle for democracy, and in the defence of democratic regimes. In fact, Marxists of all sorts were in the forefront in the struggle against Fascism in Spain, in defence of the democracy of the Republic. They played a major part in arresting the growth of Fascism in France in the 1930s. Theoretical and political errors were made, but democracy would be much weaker today if it were not for the energies of thousands of members of the Communist and Trotskyist movements.

## *Democracy and the "Mixed Economy"*

We must agree with Shirley Williams when she states that socialism can be achieved only with the consent of the majority of the population. Although she mistakenly implies that Marx and Trotsky were consistent advocates of one-party rule we share her expressed belief in the desirability of a multi-party political system in advanced capitalist democracies. She appears, on the face of it, to be a super-democrat, for we find in her speech not only a defence of *parliamentary* democracy but also support for *industrial* democracy. Unfortunately she is not very industrious in defining what she means by the latter. The truth, however, is not difficult to unearth, for she wanders from the issue of democratic forms to the question of the nature of the economic system:

> But while we find answers – and I believe we will find some of them through industrial democracy, and some through the representation of consumers at the levels at which decisions are made – we should hold to the plurality of power that is an essential distinguishing hallmark of the mixed economy. A mixed economy allows of a genuine dispersal of power to ordinary people.

Three key propositions are buried in the above statement. First, Shirley Williams believes that full and proper industrial democracy is compatible with "the mixed economy". Second, she believes that "the mixed economy" allows "plurality of power". And third, she sees this power being dispersed to "ordinary people".

What sort of world does Shirley Williams live in?

Her views on the mixed economy simply do not square up with the facts of life. Let us dare to give this Secretary of State for Education an elementary lesson about the real world in which we live. British capitalism is dominated by very few firms – a massive concentration of capital in just a few giant institutions. The top one hundred manufacturing firms account for about 46 per cent of output in that sector, and it has been predicted that their share of output will rise to around 66 per cent by 1980. Most of these firms are in private hands. Public corporations make up only 10 per cent of gross domestic product.

What sort of "plurality of power" is possible in a society with such a massive concentration of capital? Very little. In practice real economic power is concentrated in the hands of the directors and top managers of a couple of hundred firms. These people make up a very small percentage of the population. Their power is practically unrestrained. Even shareholders have, today, little practical say in the day-to-day running of the large enterprise, and the extent of share ownership is so concentrated (with the top 5 per cent of the population owning 96 per cent of all personal share capital) that even the ultimate formal power rests with a small minority of the population.

The "mixed economy" is, indeed, a strange and one-sided mixture. Despite inroads made by nationalisation and weak doses of economic management by the state, the British economy is increasingly dominated by giant privately-owned firms, controlled by an elite of managers and directors. Economic decisions which effect millions of working people, concerning their lives, their health, their families, and their environment are made by a small minority of industrial despots. Such is the "plurality of power" which we enjoy today!

We do not deny, of course, that Britain has a degree of democracy and civil liberty that, despite its inadequacy, should be protected and defended to the last. But that does not mean that we should not fight for its extension. There is a long way to go before ordinary people have significant democratic control of their social and natural environment.

### *Is Full Industrial Democracy Compatible With Private Ownership?*

Capitalists and top managers make up no more than four or five per cent of the economically active population. The self-employed amount to about ten per cent. The remainder obtain their living by selling their capacity to work by hand or by brain: they are employees on either a wage or a salary. A minority of these workers, including such people as doctors, lecturers and administrators, will have a significant degree of individual control over the pace and nature of their work. Their "middle class" social status is in part a reflection of this fact. However, the vast majority, the remaining 70 to 80 per cent, will be condemned to a dreary working life over which they have little control. The powers of the trade unions will be used, where possible, to increase wages and salaries and improve working conditions, but, as Rosa Luxemburg put it, it will be a "labour of Sisyphus" under capitalism.

Let us assume, however, that formal measures of "industrial democracy" are instituted under capitalism, giving the majority, the workers, democratic majority representation in the controlling boards of private industry. This reform would give them some immediate and realisable power over such things as the pace of work, the hiring of other workers, and so on. But would they have much control over investment, or over the nature of their product? To give them power over these matters the shareholders and financiers would have to agree to, or be compelled by the state, to provide the necessary finance and capital. Unless the range of policy options open to the workers was to be deliberately limited, in most circumstances compulsion would be necessary. We have only to recollect the venomous attacks by leading supporters of private enterprise upon the new worker co-operatives to judge the likely attitude of the ruling class to such experiments in industrial democracy – they would face an economic embargo by private capital.

It should be clear that the full flowering of industrial democracy can only take place through the *denial* of such economic power to the capitalists and large shareholders. The bourgeoisie would not like its industrial power to be limited, nor its practical redundancy to be demonstrated by the effective functioning of an economic system without their involvement. Full industrial democracy and the hegemony of private capital are incompatible, as long as the "mixture" in our "mixed economy" is as one-sided as it is.

(The above argument should not be interpreted as an attack on the noble experiments in worker control and worker cooperation in production which have taken place, and will continue to take place under capitalism. These struggles are admittedly against unfavourable odds but their educative and practical effect on the labour movement is such that they should be vigorously and actively supported. For a highly persuasive defence of such experiments see Ken Coates, "Some Questions and Some Arguments", in K. Coates (ed.) *The New Worker Cooperatives,* Spokesman, 1976).

### *State Ownership, Liberty and Democracy*

Just as there is no basis to Shirley Williams' argument that the mixed economy provides a cornucopia of freedom for the masses there is also no basis to her assertion that complete state ownership means a necessary denial of such freedom. Her assertion is based on no argument whatsoever; she simply quotes Anthony Crosland, saying:

> complete state collectivism is without question incompatible with liberty and democracy.

But the assertion should be questioned. The example of the Soviet Union, where liberty and democracy are, indeed, limited, does not show that complete state ownership is *necessarily* incompatible with liberty and democracy. In fact it has been commonplace in our movement to identify an extension of state ownership, under democratic control, with an *increase* of liberty and democracy. Even Herbert Morrison was heard to remark at Labour Party Conference 1946:

> Economic planning is the firm basis for true liberty. The socialist vision is a great libertarian conception. The deliberate organisation of material things is the only safeguard of our individual freedom . . . The British people will show the world the way to successful practical democracy – the people working for the people. *(Labour Party Annual Conference Report, 1946)*

Morrison, of course, did not strive much to have all this put into practice, as he occupied a position on the right of the Labour Party in the 1940s. But he is here clearly to the left of Shirley Williams.

It is well known that, in practice, Labour Governments have had, at most, a half-hearted attitude to extension of state ownership. But in the mainstream ideology of that Party nationalisation has rarely been seen as a *denial* of liberty and democracy, ever since the Party adopted Clause Four in 1918. The Labour Party programme of that year, *Labour and the New Social Order,* made its position clear:

> We of the Labour Party . . . must ensure that what is presently to be built up is a new social order, based . . . on a deliberately planned cooperation in production and distribution . . . not on enforced domination over subject nations, subject races, subject colonies, subject classes, or a subject sex, but in industry, as well as in government, on that equal freedom, that general consciousness of consent, and that widest participation in power which is characteristic of democracy.

The programme went on to commit itself to a policy which would "progressively eliminate the private capitalist from control of industry", to achieve "the scientific reorganisation of the nation's industry on the basis of the common ownership of the means of production", by nationalising in the first instance the railways, mines, shipping, canals, electricity and industrial insurance.

Statements such as these recur in official Labour Party policy statements from 1918 on. Despite the fact that they have not been much put into practice by Labour Governments, the only major round of nationalisation being under the 1945-50 Government, these policies are in complete contrast to the expressed views of Shirley Williams. Perhaps she has wandered into the wrong political party by mistake?

We must note, in passing, that very few socialists or communists have advocated *complete* "state collectivism". In a modern capitalist economy such as Britain, with its huge concentration of capital, it would be sufficient to nationalise just the largest few hundred companies under workers' control to ensure the dominance of socialist relations of production. There is no need to nationalise small enterprises, nor to abolish the concerns of the self employed. But this form of "mixed economy" will involve a very different "mixture" to that proposed by Shirley Williams. Instead of about 20 per cent of the economy being nationalised and the remainder being in private hands, less than 40 per cent would be run on capitalist lines. Shirley Williams advances the false alternatives of *either* "complete state collectivism" *or* the present "mixed economy". Perhaps a lesson in arithmetic would convince the Secretary of State for Education that there are more ways to divide a cake than in the proportions 80 to 20, and zero to 100.

Perhaps she will not take that lesson from the left. But she should take it from a friend and colleague on the right of the Labour Party. Let us heed the words of Roy Jenkins:

> the conclusion must be that it is quite impossible to advocate both the abolition of great inequalities of wealth and the acceptance of a one-quarter public sector and a three-quarters private sector arrangement. A mixed economy there will undoubtedly be, certainly for many decades and perhaps permanently, but it will need to be mixed in very different proportions from this. (*Pursuit of Progress*, 1953, p. 105).

But the question is not simply one of the abolition of inequality. It is also about issues supposedly dear to the heart of Shirley Williams: democracy and popular control. The fact is that if the population at large do not control the big corporations – they will certainly continue to control us. And complete public control is, as we have argued, impossible without nationalisation.

## *Socialism, Coercion and Consent*

It is a banal and inaccurate caricature to suggest, as Shirley Williams does, that Marxists eschew the process of obtaining consent. Marx, himself, repeatedly emphasised that the socialist transformation not only would have to achieve the consent of the majority of the population but also their active conscious involvement in the process of social change. The *Provisional Rules* of the First International, drafted by Marx, open with the following well-known words:

> the emancipation of the working classes must be conquered by the working classes themselves.

Marx was even over-optimistic about the process of consent when he wrote in his 1852 article on the Chartists:

> universal suffrage is the equivalent of political power for the working class of England, where the proletariat forms the large majority of the population.

Only a tiny majority of revolutionaries have ever advocated the forcible imposition of a socialist system by a minority upon a majority. Every other socialist has recognised that the *result* of such a coercive process would not and could not be socialism, but a form of totalitarian society. So the either/or choice between coercion and consent is really a red herring. Lucio Colletti, the Italian Marxist, has made a similar point:

> The alternative legality/violence is an old blind alley. The "violence" which matters is the transformation of real structures; the "legality" which counts is the consent of the majority. Both things are indispensable. For just as the structures cannot be transformed without the participation of the broad masses (what is involved is after all the installation of new social relations), so there can be no socialism without political struggle, without

> freedom of the press and the right to strike, without opposition and genuine elections. *(International,* Summer 1974, p. 5).

The real point of issue, which Shirley Williams chooses to ignore, is the question of the *defence* of a legitimate socialist government on the threat of sabotage or coup d'etat by a reactionary minority, or the threat of foreign interference or invasion. What should a socialist government do in such circumstances? Wait for the "consent" of reactionary forces? Avoid "coercion" of these minorities at all costs? It would be like fighting Nazi Germany with polite *requests* to Hitler to stop invading Europe and exterminating the Jews. It would be like defending the elected Allende regime in Chile with an appeal to the fascist generals to "consent" to the elected government. Shirley Williams mentions Chile in her article but quite clearly she has not learnt the most elementary of its lessons.

### *The Labour Party and the Armed Defence of Democratic Socialism*

The Labour Party as a whole has traditionally ignored the whole question of the need to defend, with armed forces, a legitimate democratically elected socialist regime. It has ignored the threat of possible resistance, sabotage, or coup d'etat. Instead of developing a strategy to defend an elected socialist government, the opposing poles of opinion within the party have chosen to dispute the false alternatives of "socialism now or gradually?";

"coercion or consent?", and "reform or revolution?"

But the party has been forced to face reality under the pressure of events. In the 1930s, with serious economic depression on a world scale, and rampaging fascism in Europe, some of the intellectual leaders of the Party began to discuss the realistic and central questions of socialist strategy. In 1932, in his book *The Crisis and the Constitution,* Harold Laski questioned if "evolutionary socialism (had) deceived itself in believing that it can establish itself by peaceful means within the ambit of the capitalist system . . . the road to power is far harder than Labour has, so far been led to imagine". (p. 9). In the same year, R. H. Tawney, evidently a favourite of Shirley Williams, insisted that the implementation of a socialist programme would be "a pretty desperate business". That it would immediately provoke "determined resistance" was, he held, "as certain as political facts can be". *(The Political Quarterly,* July-September 1932, p. 327). He even accepted that the privileged classes would use every "political and economic" measure to save their power, including "disaffection in the army" (p.337).

Sir Stafford Cripps was even more emphatic, in his contemporary pamphlet significantly entitled *Can Socialism Come by Constitutional Means?* he made it clear that

> the ruling class will go to almost any length to defeat Parliamentary action if the issue is the direct issue as to the continuance of their financial and political control (p. 2).

Commenting on this period, and the pronouncements by these leading figures of the Labour movement, Ralph Miliband has noted:

> These doubts as to the possibility of a smooth transition from a capitalist to a socialist society by normal constitutional and parliamentary means is an important facet of the the intellectual and ideological stirrings of the thirties. For the first time in the history of the Labour movement in the twentieth century, the notion that a parliamentary majority might not be enough to ensure a socialist transformation of society gained some currency outside the small circle of Marxists and near-Marxists who had always assumed that it would not be enough. *(Parliamentary Socialism,* p. 198).

It is not a question, therefore, of rejecting parliamentary and constitution means, but of recognising that the instrument of Parliament is not enough.

In 1936 the Left Book Club was launched. It was run by Victor Gollancz, Harold Laski, and John Strachey. Its offerings for the year 1937 included *The Labour Party in Perspective* by the leader of the Labour Party, Clement Attlee. Despite many weaknesses and ambiguities in this book he was forthright on one question:

> It is . . . no use blinking the fact that in the last resort a Government must be prepared to defend its authority if challenged by force. A Labour Government, if faced by an attempt to seize power by violence, would be bound to use all the forces at its command to protect democracy. It is, therefore, obliged to see that the armed forces upon which in the last resort its power depends are loyal, efficient, and adequate. (pp. 249-50).

Despite the lack of clarity in the above passage, particularly the imprecise use of the words "violence", "democracy" and "armed forces", at least Attlee was aware that a socialist government would have to face the question of its own armed defence.

Nine years later, Harold Laski, then chairman of the Labour Party, was to make more significant and extensive warnings during the period of the first majority Labour Government:

> Socialists ought to bear carefully in mind that the peaceful abdication of a class from that hold on the state-power by which it maintains its privileges, is one of the rarest phenomena of history . . . I should not myself argue that members of the Labour Party are entitled to complete and unbreakable confidence in constitutional methods as the road to a socialist society. *(The Secret Battalion,* 1946, pp. 19-23).

But it was perhaps Harold Laski's former collaborator on the Left Book Club, John Strachey, who had already put it in the clearest possible way in his classic book *What Are We To Do?,* published in 1938. The relevant passage is worth quoting almost in full:

> In the social struggle the choice of weapons can never be in the hands of the workers. It is always possible for the capitalists, at any stage of the struggle, to throw over democratic, constitutional methods; to substitute the bullet for the ballot. And the grimmest fact of the contemporary world is that hitherto, in every single case in which their possessions have been threatened, they have done so. When they do so the workers have no choice whatever to follow them into the new sphere of

struggle. For you cannot answer bullets with ballots, vote down a poison gas attack, nor protect your home from raiding bombers by passing resolutions . . . (It) is constantly pretended that the issue is one of evolution or revolution, peaceful methods or force and violence. This is a wholly false issue. The workers can never finally choose what methods they will use in their struggle, though they will, of course, stick to peaceful, constitutional methods so long as even the barest possibility of their use is left to them. The real issue is inescapably this: Do you accept the political and industrial struggle of the organised Labour movement as the only possible force which can lead the community out of capitalism into socialism? or do you hope, with the Fabians, to persuade the capitalists themselves into abolishing capitalism? The Fabians, so far as I am aware, never put forward any plan for gaining the consent of the capitalists to their own extinction, except their characteristic policy of permeation (pp. 96-7).

## *Shirley Williams' Four Questions*

Before we put the crucial questions again to Shirley Williams we shall do her the courtesy of answering the four questions with which she concludes her article. Most of our answers are "unequivocal".

*Question:* "Do you share our belief that our socialist objectives must be achieved by the method of democracy?"

*Answer:* Yes. Socialist objectives must be *achieved* by the method of democracy, but a socialist government "must be prepared to defend its authority if challenged by force" (Attlee).

*Question:* "Do you share our belief in the liberty

of each individual human being, in his or her right to express his opinions and religious beliefs truly and without fear of the consequences?"

*Answer:* Yes, of course. Any humane person would share this belief. Incidentally, I have yet to find a Trotskyist who would say "no" to this question; but I find that the Labour Cabinet of which you are a member, Mrs. Williams, has failed to put this "belief" into practice on the question of the unexplained expulsion of Philip Agee and Mark Hosenball from this country.

*Question:* "Are you prepared to say, so long as the system of parliamentary democracy is maintained in this country, that you will rule out violence as means to the achievement of your political ends?"

*Answer:* As long as the system of parliamentary democracy remains in this country socialists must not attack it with force. But we cannot rule out force in the *defence* of parliamentary democracy, nor in *defence* of the institutions of the labour movement.

*Question:* "Do you accept that, if the cause of socialism (as you define it) and the cause of democracy should come into conflict, you will stand by democracy".

*Answer:* Socialism is usually defined as an economic system where (1) public ownership is dominant, and where there is (2) some form of democratic public control over the economy and the political process. It is *impossible* for (2) to come into conflict with democracy as (2) involves an extension of democracy itself. Regarding (1), however, nationalisation is often opposed by the majority of people. In that case, therefore, we must work to win the agreement of the majority to the idea of the nationalisation of the commanding heights of the economy.

*Four questions to Shirley Williams*

It is now the turn of our influential Fabian "socialist" to answer some relevant questions. First, do you accept that a socialist government, and the institutions of the labour movement, must, if threatened by force, defend themselves by the same means? Second, do you agree with full industrial democracy, at least for workers in large interprises? Third, if so do you agree that this end can only be achieved by the nationalisation of those firms? Fourth, do you agree with the Roy Jenkins of 1953 that the reduction of inequality in this country can only be achieved by a significant extension of the nationalised sector?

Given the established policy positions of the Labour Party on such issues, unless Shirley Williams gives an unequivocal "yes" to all four questions we are tempted to conclude that she is way out of line with mainstream Labour Party opinion. But the Labour Party of recent years has become very tolerant of such "extremist infiltrators" as Mrs. Williams.

# The Antinomies of Perry Anderson

> 'The problem is not one of activism versus theory, but of how a group of people, with no generally shared system of theoretical concepts or political priorities, can act together to fight capitalism . . . and . . . after the most democratic internal interplay of ideas, to validate its theory in action. *The New Left* could not do this in the past. Can the *New Left Review* do it today?'
>
> Tariq Ali, *The Coming British Revolution*

Perry Anderson is one of the foremost Marxist theoreticians in Britain today. His works have a stature of scholarship and intellectual brilliance which is hardly rivalled. His two recently-published books on the development of the state (*Passages from Antiquity to Feudalism* and *Lineages of the Absolutist State*) were described by Ralph Miliband as 'an outstanding contribution to historical writing in the historical materialist mode; as Marxist historiography these volumes stand in a class apart'. His *Considerations on Western Marxism* is a remarkable essay, worthy not only in its analytical scheme and content but also in the penetrating candour of its 'Afterword'. Add to these major works a list of outstanding and vital essays in his journal *New Left Review* then it is clear that Anderson is in the vanguard of the contemporary resurgence of Marxist scholarship. As an established part of the heritage of socialist theory every student of Marxism must of necessity regard his works as indispensable reading. But the point of such an exercise must not only be to savour their rich content, but also to chart out the limits and omissions of such a magnificant corpus.

In this present essay we shall pass some critical comments on two significant works in Anderson's theoretical development. The first is 'Problems of Socialist Strategy' which appeared in the prophetic and resourceful collection of essays *Towards Socialism,* published in 1966 (edited by Perry Anderson and Robin Blackburn). The second, appearing just over a decade later, is his essay 'The Antinomies of Antonio Gramsci' in the hundredth issue of *New Left Review* (November 1976 – January 1977). Not only is the latter essay a muffled critique of the former but also they share a concern with central problems of socialist strategy, illuminated particularly by the works of Gramsci. Both essays are typical of the stature of their author. The former, for example, denoted the significance of both the student movement and the women's liberation movement well before the vast majority of British socialists, and years before these formative battalions burst into the British political scene. The latter is a major dissection of Gramsci's work on the state, which explains the acceptance of Gramsci's work by a wide and conflicting spectrum of socialists by the inherent ambiguity of its concepts.

But these are not the matters which conern us

here. We are to direct our attention to the central questions of socialist strategy which are discussed in Anderson's two essays. In particular, both of these works embody a discourse on the nature of the state in advanced capitalist countries; a matter to which strategists must pay prime attention.

### *The Two Roads to Socialism*

The 1966 essay, 'Problems of Socialist Strategy', reviews two differing strategic models for the socialist transformation:

> 'Two strategic models have dominated our history, and divided the socialist movements in Europe from the turn of the century to our own time. The momentous schism between Social-Democracy and Communism derives directly from them. They can be called the parliamentary and the insurrectionary roads to socialism.' (p.223)

The insurrectionary strategy is associated with Lenin and the experience of the October Revolution. The parliamentary strategy is found in the writings and speeches of Sidney Webb, the Fabians, and many other social-democrats. In a characteristic piece of geo-political analysis, the sort of Andersonian fusion of politics and geography that later becomes even more prominent in such works as his *Considerations,* the two roads to socialism are mapped on different sides of the cultural spine of Europe:

> 'These two conceptions became ruling visions on different sides of the great geo-political divide which runs between Western and Eastern Europe; they correspond to two worlds and two histories. In Russia and Yugos-

> lavia, Lenin's vision came true: in other Eastern European countries it was realised artificially and deformed.' (p.225).

Anderson, of course, does not omit to mention the limitations of the social revolution in thc eastern half of Europe, and the degenerated or deformed nature of the regimes that exist there today, but in a terse analysis (pp.224-9) he makes the necessary admission that it was a social revolution all the same. His rejection of Leninism in 1966 was not based on moralistic qualms but on its inapplicability to the West:

> 'Leninism, then, with all its inhuman costs, represented an immense, promethean progress for Russia, as it does today for China. But its very adaptation to its Eastern environment, which has been the secret of its success, radically *disadapts* it from the Western milieu where capitalism remains supreme today. For the societies of Western Europe constitute a wholly different universe from that of Eastern Europe, let alone Asia. Their highly advanced economies and their complex, dense, tesselated histories have created a social and cultural world entirely of its own. The great political achievement of this world has been democracy. Whatever its lacunae or limitations, this democracy represents a permanent acquisition of mankind – an experience so important that it will eventually itself become democratized, and cease to be the experience of a region. For the moment, it is important to emphasize that a Leninist strategy in the West is fundamentally *regressive:* it threatens to destroy a vital historical creation, when the task is to surpass it. And, in fact, Leninism as such has not had any success in Western Europe; it has never come near to doing so. Neither as norm nor as strategy is it an acceptable option. It is refused by the whole cultural texture of the advanced capitalist societies of the West.' (p.230)

Ten years later, as we shall see below, Anderson has arrived at a much more positive assessment of the applicability of Leninism to Western Europe.

It must be made clear, however, that in 1966 Anderson did not reject Leninism to embrace social-democracy and the parliamentary road. He followed his critique of Leninism with another terse statement on its main strategic contender. Despite electoral success the final verdict is a solemn one:

> 'The balance-sheet of sixty years of social-democracy is thus arrestingly poor. Not merely has it not brought about socialism anywhere: it has not in itself affected any major structural change in the societies in which it has acted. . . . Everything initially happened, in fact, as if social democracy was destined to be in the West what Leninism was in the East – the indigenous road to socialism. But it failed to become so. Leninism represented a sombre but genuine adaptation to its world; social-democracy represented a false adaptation. It appeared to be appropriate for its time and place, but this was not a genuine adaption, it was in fact an *absorption*.' (pp.233-4)

## *The Key Error*

Leninism was criticised for its regressive attitude to the democratic advances in the West. Then, in a highly significant section, Anderson lays bare the analytical and practical flaws within social democracy:

> 'The key error of social-democracy was a *strategic* error – a basic, ineradicable misconception of the nature of power in advanced capitalist societies and the means of attaining it. The whole *modus operandi* of social-demo-

cratic politics is geared to an illusion; it is predicated on the existence of a monocentric democracy in which power is co-extensive with the means of legislation. In this vision, society becomes a translucent, formal design, in which power is distributed symmetrically to every adult citizen at regular intervals (elections), and is then immediately reconstituted into a new, unitary pattern (government). Power exists simply as this instantaneous prestation between electorate and Parliament. The entire energies of the social-democratic party are thus polarized towards this one supreme moment; everything else is secondary. Elections become autoletic contests which apparently govern the whole fate of the nation.' (p.235)

So the cardinal sin is *electoralism.* A naive vision which the elected Parliament sits at the top of the power structure of advanced capitalist democracy. A routinist political practice in which political action is reduced simply to the mobilisation of votes.

The present-day Perry Anderson would probably not dissent from the passage of 1966 quoted above. But in all probability the same cannot be said for the account of the realities of political power which is found in the article of more than ten years ago. The common factor is a denial of the political supremacy of Parliament, but after that the articles of 1966 and 1976 differ in fundamental terms, as we shall see later when we come to compare the following passage with its later rival:

'For the reality is, of course, that power in advanced capitalist societies is not an object sited exclusively – or even primarily – in Parliament, to be passed to and fro as majorities change. It is not an object at all: *it is the totality of differential relationships that constitutes a society*. These relationships are, of course, mediated and objectified in a range of crucial institutions. These institutions are infinitely more numerous and various than Parliament. They include a myriad micro-social formations: families, schools, universities, factories, offices, newspapers, cinemas, banks, laboratories, squadrons, secretariats, etc. These formations in turn make up larger agglomerations – the great institutional orders of the society: education, economy, communications, army, bureaucracy. Parliament is among these. Each has its own specific degree of autonomy. The legislature is thus *one* of a series of sectors of power, not their synthesis. The dynamic configuration of these different ensembles is the real constellation of power in the society.' (pp.235-6)

The characteristic feature of the above passage is its failure to elucidate the *structure* of power in advanced capitalist democracies. There is nothing to avoid an *equation* of 'army' with 'education', of 'education' with 'economy', simply in terms of the efficacy of their political power. It is a rather eclectic factorial analysis; power is seen as the combination of a number of texturally dissimilar but symmetrically placed 'factors'.

This analysis is consummated in a return to the comparison between Leninism and social-democracy:

'What is the lesson of this long impasse, which over the years has altered European capitalism so little and European social-democracy so much? The answer lies within the terms of the comparison made at the beginning of this analysis. Leninism and social-democracy are apparently in every way poles apart; violence against legality, vanguardism against passivity, discipline against democracy. *Yet in one respect there is a fundamental similarity between the two. They both polarize their whole strategies on the State: civil society remains outside the main orbit of their action.* Here lies the clue to the real adaptation of the one and the false adaptation of the other. For in the East, the State was the sole vector of social action and transformation: civil society had no structured existence independent of it. To change society, Leninism in one form or another was a necessity. *But in the West, just the opposite is true.* There, in conditions of diminishing scarcity, civil society predominates politically over the State, and determines it in its image. *The heteronomy of the State is the root cause of the failure of social-democracy.*' (p.237)

'Civil society' was not clearly defined. But the implication is that it consists of such institutions as the family, schools, universities, the press and so on. It clearly is regarded as a terrain which excludes the state itself. Anderson goes on to elaborate the supremacy of civil society in Western Europe:

'It was the balance between civil society and the State which *both allowed the growth of democracy – and its confiscation by the hegemonic class, in the successful defence of capitalism.* The autonomy of civil society prevented the permanent erection of an arbitrary State, *but it also made it unnecessary.* Power was not exclusively lodged in a top-heavy, massive State machine, whose democratization would *de facto* threaten to revolutionize the whole existing social order. It was diffused through the whole variegated, supple, intricate texture of civil society. It was the invisible colour of daily life itself. In these conditions, there was little risk of revolutionary consequences from parliamentary democracy. The history of social-democracy has offered an endless demonstration of this truth.' (p.239)

## *Civil Society and the State*

In the Anderson of 1966, therefore, the fundamental difference in the structure of power between Western and Eastern Europe was this: in the West civil society 'predominates politically' over the state, in the East the order of supremacy is reversed and the limited weight of civil society is far exceeded by that of the state machine. Anderson's later work has supplied an analytical and convincing correction to this earlier depiction. In his *Lineages of the Absolutist State* he comes to the following conclusion regarding the Russia of the Tsars:

> 'there was a *dislocation* between the social formation and State in the last years of Tsarism. The Russian *social formation* was a complex ensemble dominated by the capitalist mode of production, but the Russian *State* remained a feudal Absolutism.' (p.353)

It is not the political predominance of the state which is singled out as a key difference here: it is the different nature of the state itself. Before 1917 Russia was capitalist social formation *without* a capitalist state – a monolithic feudal autocracy occupied its place. Not only is the state predominant, but it is a type of state in essential contrast to that found in the West. The conclusion must be clear: Russia neither before nor after the Revolution experienced the implantation of a capitalist state proper. It passed from a feudal absolutism through a workers' state to some form of degenerate post-capitalist autocracy, later modified, after the death of Stalin, to an oligarchy. Such oligarchic power now stretches from the Elbe to the Pacific. Over that wide area capitalist state power has had no perceptible indigenous influence.

The Andersonian geo-political map remains intact in 1976. What has been altered is the justification for its frontiers. In his recent essay on Gramsci the old view of the predominance of civil society over the state in the West is renounced. Although, 'culture' remains dominant in the *normal* day to day life of Western democracies the role of violence is 'fundamental' or 'determinant' (*New Left Review* 100, p.42). Whenever this normalcy is challenged, i.e. bourgeois class rule is threatened, as in a revolutionary crisis, violence changes its position in the configuration of power, and moves to the forefront:

> 'For historically, and this is the most essential point of all, the development of a revolutionary crisis necessarily displaces the dominance within the bourgeois power structure from ideology to violence. Coercion becomes both *determinant and dominant* in the supreme crisis, and the army inevitably occupies the front of the stage in any class struggle against the prospect of a real inauguration of socialism . . . In fact, any revolutionary crisis within an advanced capitalist country must inevitably produce a reversion to the ultimate determinant of the power system: force. This is a law of capitalism, which it cannot violate, on pain of death. It is the rule of the end-game situation.' (*Ibid.*, p.44).

Capitalist power in the West, therefore, embodies the feature of all developed capitalist political systems: a 'mobile' centre of power constituted by force. In the East, with no capitalist *political* heritage of significance, this centre is relatively immobile, and thus remains close to the borders of normalcy.

### *The Analysis of Parliamentary Democracy*

We cannot contest Anderson's 1976 statement on the ultimate role of force. It is an important correction to his earlier statements. We turn now to another decadal shift of position: on the question of parliamentary democracy. The 1966 article has little to say on the purpose or desirability of socialist representation in Parliament. Instead, we are asked to subordinate the electoral process to a political offensive within civil society:

> '*In effect, socialist strategy must aim at entering and inhabiting civil society at every possible point, establishing an entire alternative system of power and culture within it.*' (p.279)

What is the means by which such an alternative can be built up? What is the social force upon which its success must rely? The answer is provided in several statements, two of which are reproduced below:

> 'The whole strategy discussed above depends upon one immense precondition: a socialist ideology. Without this, the entire range of possible actions and initiatives has no meaning. For by definition, there is no possibility whatever of ending capitalist hegemony in Britain by purely political or organizational moves. This hegemony rests on a total vision of the world – and can only be replaced by another vision of the world.' (p.282)

And elsewhere:

'The battle for the working class can, as have seen, only be won on the plane of ideology.' (p.265)

The analysis of parliamentary democracy, and its place in a strategy of socialist change, is, in 1966, conspicuous only by its *absence.* Instead, the decisive battles take place in the sphere of civil society, with ideas as ammunition. Parliament, by implication, has no significant positive or negative role in the clash of ideologies.

The contrast with his later position is graphic. After summarising his 1966 position on the need to give priority to the battle of ideas, before electoral or political moves, in the sphere of civil society alone, he produces a remarkable and self-critical analysis, referring to his earlier position as a variant or 'left social-democracy'. The political illusions of this current now draw his fire. According to 'left social-democracy':

'the main task of socialist militants is not combat with an armed State, but ideological conversion of the working class to free it from submission to capitalist mystifications. This characteristic syndrome of left social-democracy contains a number of illusions. The first and most immediate of its errors is precisely the notion that the ideological power of the bourgeoisie in Western social formations is exercised above all in the sphere of civil society, its hegemony over which subsequently neutralizes the democratic potential of the representative State. The working class has access to the State (elections to parliament), but does not exercise it to achieve socialism because of its indoctrination by the means of communication. In fact, it might be said that the truth is if anything the inverse: the general form of the representative state – bourgeois democracy – is itself the principal ideological lynchpin of Western capitalism, whose very existence deprives the working class of the idea of socialism as *a different type of State*, and the means of communication and other mechanisms of cultural control thereafter clinch this central ideological 'effect' . . . The bourgeois State thus by definition 'represents' the totality of the population, *abstracted* from its distribution into social classes, as individual and equal citizens. In other words, it presents to men and women their unequal positions in civil society as if they were equal in the State. Parliament, elected every four or five years as the sovereign expression of popular will, reflects the fictive unity of the nation back to the masses as if it were their own self government . . . The existence of the parliamentary State thus constitutes the formal framework of all other ideological mechanisms of the ruling class. It provides the general code in which every specific message elsewhere is transmitted. The code is all the more powerful because the juridical rights of citizenship are not a mere mirage: on the contrary, the civic freedoms and suffrages of bourgeois democracy are a tangible reality, whose conception was historically in part the work of the labour movement itself, and whose loss would be a momentous defeat for the working class.' (p.28)

The forceful and brilliant auto-polemic in the passage above contains a number of positive achievements. First, it is a clear break from the 'ideologism' of his earlier position; in which the battle of ideas is the fundamental and decisive contest in social change. Instead, we have an appropriate recognition of the status and determining role of institutions, Parliament in particular. The concrete role of such an institution in generating, reproducing and 'reflecting' the illusions of bourgeois liberalism is acknowledged. Second, another implication is clear; it is the state that dominates civil society, not civil society the state. The 'silence' on the question of Parliament in 1966 is now filled with a loud proclamation of its functional centrality in perpetrating the stability of the bourgeois order.

## *The Question of Socialist Strategy*

In my view this analysis of parliamentary democracy is the high point of Anderson's essay on Gramsci. On reading beyond that point there are many valid points and rich morsels of analysis, but in the same way as the conspicuous silence on the question of Parliament in the 1966 essay steals the air, another loud void protrudes above the rest of the composition. The absence is one of *practical socialist strategy.* In a few passages a vain attempt is made to fill this vacuum, the mention of the 'united front' for example. But they are on a too abstract and non-immediate level to be of practical use. For two reasons this omission is remarkable. First, the object of his discourse, the writings of Antonio Gramsci, contain many rich illuminations on this question. Anderson's critique of this theorist is confined to the latter's views on the nature of the state and its relation to civil society, and Gramsci's *most abstract* strategic imperatives, e.g. the counterposition of the 'war of position' to the 'war of manoeuvre'. Yet Gramsci's writings are filled with much more of direct use on the question. *The Modern Prince,* for example, is a superb attempt to develop a methodology of revolutionary action. At a more concrete level, Gramsci's discussions of Italian history and the formation of intellectuals are clearly geared to the central questions of building popular alliances with diverse strata of the population and forging an effective revolutionary socialist party.

Second, the omission of the question of strategy is remarkable because of the awareness in the 1976 essay of the influence of its progenitor of ten years before. In the earlier essay, despite its acknowledged faults, there is a wealth of immediate practical suggestions. The essay may be faulted for its submission to the famous classic reformist motif of Eduard Bernstein: 'The movement is everything, the final goal is nothing'. In the 1976 essay, in contrast, these words are stood on their head: the final goal is everything the movement is nothing. The result is no strategy, no movement.

If we attempt a 'reading' of Anderson's analysis which poses the key questions of immediate socialist strategy then we may be forced to an unacceptable conclusion. Consider the key passage on parliamentary democracy, quoted above. It explains, correctly, the role of Parliament in providing the framework in which bourgeois ideology constructs its hold upon the masses. The stabilising role of this institution is explained. What, then, follows from this analysis? At first sight if Parliament is such a key institution in maintaining bourgeois power then there is no way to socialism without smashing or removing it. But this is the very ultra-leftist error that Anderson is keen to renounce. He arrests the logic of his discourse with the remark that the loss of 'bourgeois democracy' would be 'a momentous defeat for the working class'. The conclusion, therefore, appears to be this: no passage to socialism is possible without the removal of Parliament, yet the cost of this prior removal is unacceptable, so the road to socialism itself is *impassable.* The costs of the transformation to socialism in advanced capitalist democracies are too great to bear. We must pessimistically resign ourselves to the fact of the supremacy of the bourgeois order in the West.

Yet I am sure that Anderson, himself, would not want to share in such pessimism. In the later pages of his essay on Gramsci he makes evident his current view that the revolutionary tradition of Lenin and Trotsky is the one that provides the strategic route for the socialist transformation, even in the western half of Europe. Yet Lenin and Trotsky did make it clear that 'bourgeois democracy', including Parliament, would have to be *smashed.* Socialists should use the electoral and parliamentary apparatus under capitalism to make propaganda only: not to attempt to make fundamental changes in the system, as these would be made by the armed and led masses themselves, on the basis of soviet-style institutions. This espousal of classic Leninism and Trotskyism is inconsistent with the slim statement that the loss of bourgeois democracy and Parliament would be a 'momentous defeat'. How, then, do we interpret the latter statement? The conclusion is inescapable. This single, limited, evaluation of Parliament as a positive institution is a 'token clause' designed to repel any charge of ultra-leftism. To turn Anderson's indictment of Gramsci against

Anderson himself: 'Against his own intention, formal conclusions can be drawn from his work that lead away from revolutionary socialism' (p.72) – and towards the mire of the impotent, sloganising, far-left grouplets. The single, insufficient, 'token clause' is not enough to camouflage Anderson's real present positon.

In his 1966 essay, as we have seen, Anderson counterposed the two strategies of the 'insurrectionary' and the 'parliamentary' roads to socialism. But then he attempted to transcend them both. Now is he *en route* down the insurrectionary road. Parliament is to be counterpoised in a situation of 'dual power' and replaced by insurgent 'proletarian democracy'. What his present position has in *common* with that of 1966 is a neglect of any consideration of Parliament as an arena for strategic operations. He has reached a simple *inversion* of the Kautskyite reformism that he has correctly been keen to criticise. The weakness of Kautsky's position, as Anderson notes, is his subordination of mass struggle to the contest in Parliament. But Kautsky is 'sophisticated' enough to provide a 'token clause' which talks of the need for a 'mass strike' in the far-off future to clinch proletarian power in the apocalyptic showdown with capital. For the day-to-day struggle extra-parliamentary action is effectively devalued. Anderson's inversion has an ironic symmetry. Parliament cannot be a major area for socialist struggle; it cannot be a strategic focus, for Anderson now accepts the road of pure insurrection. Yet his 'token clause' is there, as we have noted: the loss of Parliament would be a 'momentous defeat'. What is missing, of course, from the views of both Anderson and Kautsky is a *dual strategy* which effectively combines both extra-parliamentary and parliamentary action, for they are *both essential* for a socialist revolution in the West. Way back in 1966 it seemed that Anderson had *started* to develop such a strategy, despite the acknowledged weaknesses of this earlier essay. The tragedy is that, in *strategic* terms, he has got no further.

### *The Search for Panaceas*

The closing pages of Anderson's essay on Gramsci read like a frantic search for panaceas. The first such panacea is the Trotskyist mantle. Trotsky, himself, makes a strange entrance, not as a brilliant analyst of *political* conjunctures, but as a renowned *military* theorist. On purely *military* grounds he is used as a critic of the false counterposition of the 'war of manoeuvre' with the 'war of position' in warfare (pp.72-5). The applicability, however, of military theory to the realm of politics is left in doubt. Gramsci, himself, remarked that all military-political analogies must be taken 'with a pinch of salt' (*Prison Notebooks,* London 1971, p.231). So too must Anderson's invocation of Trotsky's military writings; despite their military value they cannot be artificially transposed to politics without severe qualification.

When Anderson comes to discuss Trotsky's politics it is accepted that while

'Trotsky's historical command of the specific sociopolitical structures of capitalism in the central countries of Western Europe had no equal in his own time, he never posed the problem of a differential strategy for making the socialist revolution in them, unsheduled by that in Russia, with the same anxiety or lucidity as Gramsci.' (p.75)

But that is as far as it goes. Anderson never poses more than a Trotskyist strategy for the West. He does not even hesitate when reeling out this passage from Trotsky's *Where is Britain Going?* where the author is discussing the scenario of a classic Russian-style proletarian insurrection in Britain:

> 'The workers must in advance take all measures to draw the soldiers to the side of the people by means of preliminary agitation; but at the same time they must forsee that the government will always be left with a sufficient number of dependable or semi-dependable soldiers for them to call out for the purposes of quelling an insurrection' (Quoted on p.77).

What is wrong with this passage is *not* the implication that force and coercion are determinant in the last instance, neither is it incorrect to observe that in Britain reactionary armed forces could be mobilised against the people in the event of an incipient socialist transformation. The fault is the automatic presumption that 'the government will always' be *against* such a transformation and be the mobiliser of reactionary armed force. In fact, a far more likely scenario in Britain is that the socialist transformation will be *preceded* and *accompanied* by a period of *left government.* In the event of a social upheaval even an equivocating left government could be forced, with sufficient extra-parliamentary agitation, to act with and for the socialist masses. Having removed the threat of reactionary force by a combination of extra-parliamentary organisation, mobilisation, and struggle, with parliamentary legitimation, fundamental changes could be made in the political and economic structures, and the construction of socialism could be commenced.

Anderson adopts a quite different scenario, even for the advanced capitalist democracies of Western Europe. It is quite simply the strategy of *dual power,* originated by Lenin to deal with the realities of Russia 1917 and promulgated as an idea by Trotsky until his death. Anderson writes:

> 'Such a revolution will only occur in the West when the masses have made the experience of a proletarian democracy that is tangibly superior to bourgeois democracy. The sole way for the victory of socialism to be secured in these societies is for it to represent incontestably more, not less, freedom for the vast majority of the population. It is the untapped store of popular energies that any inception of a real workers' democracy would thereby release, that will provide the explosive force capable of ending the rule of capital. For the exhibition of a new, unprivileged liberty must start before the old order is structurally cancelled by the conquest of the State. The name of this necessary overlap is dual power.' (p.78)

This quotation is from the last page of Anderson's recent essay. The voyage from pessimistic analysis to the panacea of dual power is complete. Yet there is not a hint of the method of construction of such a dual configuration of power, neither is there any expressed optimism in their automatic emergence, and that would have been inappropriate even if it were present. The viability of 'proletarian democracy' is simply asserted, the possibility of 'dual power' is simply affirmed. Yet, for decade after decade neither have emerged in any advanced capitalist democracy. The scenario of 'dual power' has never been fully enacted in the advanced capitalist West. In another work Anderson wrote of the Trotskyist movement:

> 'Reaffirmation of the validity and reality of socialist revolution and proletarian democracy, *against so many events which denied them,* involuntarily inclined this tradition towards conservatism. The preservation of classical doctrines took priority over their development.' (*Considerations on Western Marxism,* pp.100-1, emphasis inserted.)

To what extent can this charge be now levelled against Anderson himself?

### *Myths of Dual Power*

Contrary to a myth of the present Marxist left, the emergence of Soviets in Russia was not a completely spontaneous event. In fact, the original iniative to form a Soviet in St. Petersburg in 1905 came from the Tsar! Isaac Deutscher described the birth of the first Soviet in the following words:

> 'The workers clamoured for constitutional freedom as well as for better wages and shorter hours. As the (October) strike developed there sprang into being an institution bred in the bone of the Russian Revolution: the first Council, or Soviet, of Workers' Deputies. The

> Soviet was not a Bolshevik invention . . . The nucleus of the Soviet was set up by the strikers from fifty printing shops, who elected delegates and instructed them to form a council. These were soon joined by delegates of other trades. Paradoxically, the idea itself had, indirectly and unwittingly, been suggested by the Tsar who, after the events of January, had appointed a commission under a Senator Shydlovsky to investigate the causes of the trouble. The commission had ordered the workers to elect their representatives from the factories in order to voice grievances. The strikers in October followed this precedent. When the Soviet first met, on 13 October, only delegates of one district (the Neva district) attended. A stimulus was needed to induce other districts to join in. That stimulus was provided by the Mensheviks, who would one day bitterly oppose the institution to which they now acted as godfathers.' (*The Prophet Armed,* New York, pp.125-6)

It is clear that even in absolutist Russia there was a profound interaction between the rising institutions of working-class power and the established order. If the Soviets emerged in Russia in a clamour for constitutional reform, and with the initial impetus of apparent Tsarist legitimation, then the links with the given constitutional order will be greater and not less if such institutions emerge in an advanced capitalist democracy. The links under an autocracy are limited by the nature of such a social system. The Tsarist State, for example, was a feudal autocracy perched on a quite different social formation. Mass politics were beyond its grasp. As mass struggle intensified, popular organs of power, such as Soviets, and even Parliament itself, were forced into direct and open confrontation with that state. In the case of the Tsarist

Duma, or Parliament, its functioning was always severely constricted, and sometimes suspended. Hence the Soviets in 1905, after a period of pressuring for reform of the existing state, were rapidly forced into an insurrectionary posture. In an autocracy, mass popular organs of power must inevitably be forced into direct confrontation, because of both the real and apparent detachment of the autocracy from the masses themselves. Dual power, therefore, in the particular form that it appeared in Russia, was highly structured by the nature of the apparatus of political and state power in that country.

If dual power emerges in a country such as Britain then it will be of a quite different nature. If soviet-style organs of power were to emerge then their connections with the existing constitutional order would be of much greater intensity. The dialectic of institutions between soviets, Parliament, and the armed forces will not quickly and inevitably explode into a conflict of force between the masses and the entire state apparatus. In fact, as Ken Coates has remarked, if soviets were ever to emerge in Britain then it would be, in all likelihood, in defence of the rights and prerogatives of Parliament to implement key reforms, against the actions of, for example, the House of Lords, the Civil Service, or the armed forces. The real situation may be that Parliament is, in fact, continually detached from the masses in its exercise of power. But appearances are to the contrary. As Anderson himself remarks in his essay on Gramsci:

> 'For the peculiarity of the historical consent won from the masses within modern capitalist social formations is by no means to be found in its mere secular reference or technical awe. The novelty of this consent is that it takes the fundamental form of a belief by the masses that *they exercise an ultimate self-determination* within the existing social order. It is thus not acceptance of the superiority of an acknowledged ruling class (feudal ideology), but credence in the democratic equality of all citizens in the government of the nation – in other words, disbelief in the existence of any ruling class.' (p.30)

Thus the *appearance* of the classlessness and equality of parliamentary representation within capitalism becomes a prop within the existing social order. The cognition of apparent democratic equality becomes a *real* social force. The appearance, itself, in a sense, is real.

There are few historical examples to illustrate the close relations between Parliament and mass institutions of popular power in advanced capitalist democracies. This is because such institutions have rarely emerged in the Western democracies in the last half a century. One example worth mention is the emergence of Councils of Action in the British General Strike of 1926. Despite the fact that the furtherance of the strike was bound to bring clashes with the police and armed forces, a struggle of insurrectionary proportions never began to develop, nor was it likely to do so. The links between the mass struggle and the established order were illustrative in a rather negative sense, due to the unequivocal opposition of the Conservative Government to the strike. The defeat of the strike was not just a result of the betrayal of the trade union leaders, nor of the opposition of the Government. The social forces behind the characters in the conflict must also be unmasked. Defeat of the struggle was partially a result of the ability of the Government to convince many people, including trade unionists, that the strike was a threat to the democratic and apparently egalitarian constitutional order. For that reason a general strike against private capital would have had a much greater chance of success if it were backed by a more radical government.

Legislation is clearly not a pre-requisite for workers' struggle, as the working class will always show a capacity for independent initiatives in industry. But legislation can have a galvanising effect on large numbers of workers in certain circumstances. In the USA in the 1930s the National Industrial Recovery Act apparently gave the workers the 'right to belong to a union'. This legislation legitimated the CIO's massive industrial unionisation drive in large industry, leading to bitter clashes with the employers, and occupations of several factories. On the whole the unionisation drive was successful, and the firm establishment of trades unionism in the USA dates from that period. Without the backing of the legislation of the Federal Government, albeit a bourgeois government, it is doubtful if the struggle would have been as successful.

The experience of fascism in the 1930s can, paradoxically, provide us with some clues as to how an interaction of mass struggle and constitutional power can achieve a socialist revolution. Fascism, of course, is reactionary and regressive, but it does rely on a mass movement. Yet it could not achieve its aims by pure insurrection, despite attempts to do this in both Italy and Germany. Its road to power was through a bloody dialectic with the existing order. As G.D.H. Cole wrote many years ago:

> 'It is noteworthy that even Mussolini and Hitler made large use of constitutional forms in carrying through their several revolutions. Mussolini, indeed, began with the revolutionary action of the "March on Rome"; but thereafter he was careful to execute his policy as far as possible in formal consistency with the law of the Italian Constitution. Hitler actually came to power in the guise of a constitutional Prime Minister, at the head of a Coalition Government. Both used the Constitution, whever it was usable, to give formal sanction to what were in essence clearly revolutionary acts and policies.' (*The Meaning of Marxism,* 1964 ed., p.203.)

These observations on reactionary fascism in Europe are used to support the viability of a positive interaction between a socialist mass movement and a socialist government:

> 'in countries equipped with powerful parliamentary institutions, the transition (to socialism) can and should begin as a constitutional movement, and thereafter develop into a social revolution under the aegis of the constitutional authority under which it has begun.' (*Ibid.*)

It should be added, of course, that a socialist movement is likely to meet the resistance of the armed forces. For that reason the movement must create the means of removing and defeating the threat of reactionary force, by armed force in return if necessary. But that does not undermine Cole's picture of the socialist transformation: the socialist movement will be all the more effective if it has constitutional authority behind it.

### *Winning Over the Workers*

Yet in Anderson's 1976 essay the roles of constitutional authority and parliamentary legitimation are not recognised. In the closing paragraphs of his article, from the point where he raises the question of the contemporary relevance of past debates to socialist strategy, he degenerates into near-banality. We are told, once again, that a socialist revolution must, at some stage, involve a conflict of force with those elements of the police and army which will not be won over to the cause. All that is worth saying. But where does it leave us? Apart from the invocation of the tactic of the united front we are told little else than this:

> 'The imperative need remains to win the working class, before there can be any talk of winning power.' (p.78)

But how? The slogan of the 'united front', is our only, unexplained, answer.

So here we come to the second crucial silence of Anderson's whole work. It is what has been termed, by C. Wright Mills and others, an analysis of the *problem of agency of social change.* In the 1966 essay the problem of agency was approached in an oblique, limited, but positive fashion. He seemed to suggest that the main agency for socialism in Britain, at least for the moment, was the Labour Party. But this point is never made explicit nor discussed, and this major silence is compounded in his 1976 article. Here the agency of socialist change is simply 'the working class' – abstract, diffuse, unstructured, unorganised, unrelated to their historical institutions and those of the alien world around them. There is nothing to prevent us falling into the idealist and syndicalist trap of envisaging the working class as a near-united elemental force acting independently of the institutional and social culture. In reality, however, the picture is different. There is no abstract 'working class' independent of the trade unions, political parties, informal and formal organisation in the workplace, and all the elements of working class sub-culture. Working class consciousness cannot emerge automatically from the daily struggle between labour and capital at work, as Lenin pointed out many years ago. The mechanisms of its emergence are those very institutions to which we refer. And we cannot talk of a working class unless such a consciousness has begun to emerge. So to pose the working class as the agent of socialist change, although correct in the abstract, does not answer the concrete problem of agency. That answer can only be found in an examination of the structures of power and the real connecting mechanisms between the masses under capitalism – and it was Gramsci who was one of the first to see the urgency and centrality of that task.

We can briefly note that, in our view, Parliament plays a key role in the generation of the consciousness of the masses, especially in advanced capitalism. Anderson, too, is aware of this point. But because he fails to place it in the context of a search for the agency of social change he does not recognise the role that Parliament may play in developing a mass popular socialist movement. Of course, that movement will have to rely on much else besides Parliament, as that alone cannot be an agent of major social change. But besides recognising the negative and stultifying role that Parliament plays in times of normalcy, the positive potential of that institution when fused with a massive and energetic socialist movement has to be recognised. Both a socialist majority in Parliament and a mass socialist movement are each *necessary* but not *sufficient* conditions for the socialist transformation. And as we have remarked elsewhere, it is a *result* of the correct observation that all political change resolves ultimately into a question of force that we must recognise the importance of a socialist majority in Parliament. Without that majority reactionary forces can use Parliament as a nobiliser for a *military* showdown; with it the forces of the left will be augmented and those of the right reduced.

## *The United Front*

It is this absence of a discussion of the problem of socialist agency that renders Anderson's final panacea, the united front, virtually useless. A united front, yes; but by who? with whom? for what? We are told nothing. What is the prime mover of such a front? The readers of *New Left Review*? Who are thcy uniting with? We hardly dare ask. What are they uniting for? Ah yes, to 'win over the workers'. We are in the abstract world of cookery-book slogans. We are in the street market of second-hand shibboleths. In fact, it is an impotent isolation rather than an effective urge to unite that is betrayed. For the united front is a code-phrase in the ghetto of revolutionary far-left politics. It serves a dual purpose in the hidden language of this small milieu: first a sign of the cross at the shrines of Lenin and Trotsky, for it was they who played the historical role in the application and development of the slogan, and second, a murmur to the brethren of the International Marxist Group, who have played a key and commendable role in popularising the slogan, that Anderson is on their side. The contemporary relevance of the united front panacea, in the maze of British far-left politics, cannot be ignored.

Anderson shares his trajectory, from being a Marxist within the mainstream labour movement to the relative isolation of the far-left grouplets, with a whole generation of socialists in Britain. The tragedy of this useless exodus is made more intense in that it involves a man of intellectual brilliance. But at last the weakness of his position is clear. The united front slogan is the sign of a near-desperate urge to engage his analytical genius with the cogwheels of reality. But it is the size of the cog, and its connection with the mechanisms of working class struggle that matters. Anderson cannot have failed to notice the futility and isolation of the groups on the far left, despite their hyperactivism. They are cogs without a purchase on reality.

This is not the place to discuss the need for socialists to work within the Labour Party in Britain. The case for that orientation to the mainstream of the Labour movement is well presented in Ken Coates' pamphlet *Socialists and the Labour Party.* But it ought to be acknowledged by those that, like Anderson, are in flirtation with Trotskyism, that Trotsky, himself, gave strong reasons for joining the Labour Party. These reasons still appear to be valid today:

> 'while it is necessary for the revolutionary party to maintain its independence at all times, a revolutionary grouping of a few hundred workers is not a revolutionary party and can work most effectively at present by opposition to the social patriots within the mass parties.' (*Trotsky's Writings on Britain,* p.141.)

## *The Beginnings of an Alternative*

The far-left in Britain thrives on the absence of a coherent and effective revolutionary socialist alternative within the Labour Party itself. The small 'entrist' groups with their maximalist and propagandistic posture are hardly an adequate locus of attraction. An alternative must provide a realistic strategy designed to *unlock the power structure* of the British political system, partly based on an analysis of the British state. As we have seen, Anderson has made an important contribution to this analysis, but he falls short of extending this work into the strategical terrain.

It is in recent years that the beginnings of this 'unlocking' strategy have emerged within the Labour Party, with the proposals of Planning Agreements and a National Enterprise Board, for example. Such proposals, if fully implemented in an undiluted form, can encourage a powerful interaction between mass struggle and legislative advance, and thus develop a movement to accomplish the socialist transformation. The problem of agency would be solved. The united front would have a real and meaningful object.

It must be recognised, however, that the developing economic strategy of the Labour left is not yet matched by a complete strategy to deal with the problems of transfer of political power, and the threat of reactionary repression and force. It has been traditional, as Anderson pointed out in 1966, to wrongly regard Parliament as the real locus of ultimate power in advanced capitalist democracies. Despite our emphasis on the importance of Parliament we have not fallen into this error. But even the most far-sighted and able of the strategic theorists of the Labour left have not broken from the heritage of social-democracy. Stuart Holland, for example, has been an exceedingly creative innovator as far as economic strategy goes. Yet his position on the state remains weak, as is evidenced by chapters 5 and 6 of his book *The Socialist Challenge.* Despite the strategic insights within the sphere of the economy, this section perpetrates the old confusions: the false Fabian counter-position of 'force and violence' to 'peaceful democratic pressure', the purely moralistic rejection of force – they are there. Yet, paradoxically, Holland provides, I believe, the only effective strategy of advance which at the present time can be followed. No doubt, when we come to the position of the seizure of power, a complete revolutionary change at the *political* level, Holland's Fabian errors will have to be cast aside, if not before.

It is in the writings of Holland and Anderson that the strategic thinking of the left in Britain is summed up. They together represent the antinomies of the socialist movement today, in their most articulately-expressed form. Anderson's focus is on the ultimate realities of power, Holland's on the practical realities of advance in the existing situation. They both invert and complement each other. It is quite possible, if the errors of each were corrected, that their intellectual wedlock could set the scene for the development of a comprehensive socialist strategy. A strategy which springs from the present, and prepares for the conflicts of the future.

In the meantime, we must bring back the lost sheep of the labour movement, who have strayed under the call of the sophisticated but impotent intellectualisms of Anderson's journal. We ask, with Tariq Ali: can the *New Left Review* do it?

# The Communist Party and Parliamentary Democracy

'Between the idea
And the reality
Between the motion
And the act
Falls the Shadow . . .
Between the conception
And the creation
Between the emotion
And the response
Falls the Shadow'

T.S. Eliot, *The Hollow Men*

The spectre of the Communist Party of Great Britain has indeed haunted the Labour movement since 1920. The history of that Party is well documented. We do not attempt to write another such history, nor to investigate the causes of the various changes of line that have occurred in the Party. It is our aim to examine the contrasting positions that the Party has taken on the question of parliamentary democracy, leading up to the recent revisions in the *British Road to Socialism.*

## *The Foundation of the Communist Party*

Two questions dominated the debate at the Communist Unity Convention, the founding conference of the CPGB, on the last day of July and the first of August 1920. Almost the whole of the first day was devoted to discussion of a resolution on the desirability and purpose of Communist participation in elections to Parliament. The bulk of the second day was occupied with a debate on the desirability of affiliation to the Labour Party. These two questions, to which so much time was devoted in 1920, have dominated discussions within the CPGB ever since. In fact after half a century of existence that Party has still failed to resolve them in practical terms.

During 1919 and 1920 it seemed to many Marxists in Britain that a revolution was imminent. Many of the delegates to the Unity Convention voiced this prediction in their speeches. Yet the founding conference of the most influential Marxist party in Britain did not disucss the economic trajectory of capitalism in Britain, nor the balance of class forces, nor the organisation of the working class, nor the instruments of revolution, nor the morale and strength of the bourgeoisie. They discussed participation in parliamentary elections and the desirability of affiliation to the Labour Party. As it happened, elections were to happen far more often than revolutionary situations in the next 50 years.

## *Lenin's Position*

A few days before the Convention extracts from

Lenin's newly-published *Left Wing Communism – An Infantile disorder* appeared in the left press; Lenin argued both for participation in Parliament and for affiliation to the Labour Party. However, his position was more complex than that. In this and other works Lenin saw Soviet-style proletarian democracy and 'bourgeois' parliamentary democracy as mutually exclusive. Parliament was to be utilised as a forum for Communist ideas, as a way to speak to the masses. But, most emphatically, it was not to be regarded as a positive instrument of social change. This point was made most clearly in his *State and Revolution.* In reply to Kautsky who had argued for 'a shifting of the balance of forces within the state power' and the 'winning of a majority in Parliament', Lenin wrote of such 'opportunism':

> 'We, however, shall break with the opportunists; and the entire class-conscious proletariat will be with us in the fight – not to "shift the balance of forces", but to *overthrow the bourgeoisie, to destroy* bourgeois parliamentarism, for a democratic republic after the type of the Commune, for a republic of Soviets of Workers' and Soldiers Deputies, for the revolutionary dictatorship of the proletariat'.

In conformity with Lenin's ideas a motion was moved at the Communist Unity Convention:

> 'The Communist Party repudiates the reformist view that a social revolution can be achieved by the ordinary methods of parliamentary democracy, but regards parliamentary and electoral action as a valuable means of propaganda and agitation towards the revolution . . . '

After an overwhelming vote for the resolution an amendment deleting the word 'valuable' was carried without discussion. Another resolution was passed in support of the objective of a Soviet-style government rather than a parliamentary democracy:

> 'The Communists in conference assembled declare for the Soviet (or Workers' Council) system as the means whereby the working class shall achieve power and take control of the forces of production; declare for the dictatorship of the proletariat as a necessary means for combatting the counter-revolution during the transition period between capitalism and communism . . . '

### *The Second Comintern Congress*

The Second Congress of the Communist International, meeting in August 1920, codified the position on parliamentary democracy in more detail. As the Comintern was 'democratic centralist' in structure, its position was, of course, binding on all national Communist Parties, including the newly-formed CPGB.

Twenty theses on 'communism, the fight for the dictatorship of the proletariat, and the utilization of bourgeois parliaments' were adopted. These theses had the support of CPGB member J.T. Murphy, but were opposed by William Gallacher (not yet a Party member but later, in 1935, to become a Communist Member of Parliament). The introduction to these theses, written by Trotsky, argued for participation in parliamentary institutions but it set severe limits to such participation:

> 'The attitude of the Communist International towards

parliament is determined not by any new theory, but by the change in the role of parliaments themselves. In the preceding epoch parliament, as the instrument of developing capitalism, accomplished work which was to a certain extent historically progressive. In present conditions of unbridled imperialism, however, parliament has become an instrument of falsehood, deception, violence, an enervating talk-shop . . . For communists, parliament today can in no circumstances serve as the centre of the struggle for reforms, for improving the lot of the working class, as it did at certain times in the preceding epoch. The centre of gravity of political life has been completely and finally removed beyond the confines of parliament'. *(The Communist International,* ed. J. Degras, vol.1, p.151).

The theses themselves, drafted by Bukharin, included the following propositions:

'The proletariat needs no parliamentary division of powers, which is harmful to it. The form taken by the proletarian dictatorship is the Soviet republic. Bourgeois parliaments, one of the most important pieces of machinery in the bourgeois state apparatus, cannot as such be won permanently, just as the proletariat cannot win the bourgeois State . . . The mass struggle is an entire system of developing actions which become more and more acute in form and logically lead to insurrection against the capitalist State. In this mass struggle which develops into civil war, the leading party of the proletariat must as a rule secure all legal positions, using them as auxiliary centres of its revolutionary activity and incorporating them in its main plan of campaign, the campaign of mass struggle. One such auxiliary centre is the rostrum of the bourgeois parliament. It is no argument against participation in the parliamentary struggle that parliament is a bourgeois State institution. The communist party does not enter this institution to function there as an organic part of parliament, but in order by action inside parliament to help the masses to shatter the State machine and parliament itself'. (Ibid., pp.152-3).

## *Applying Leninism in Britain*

The opposition of Gallacher and a few others to the Comintern theses was not from the right but from the left. No objection was raised to the goal of helping 'the masses to shatter the State machine and parliament itself'. Gallacher was then opposed to participation in parliamentary elections, of even using Parliament merely as a 'rostrum'. That was the main question of debate. The overwhelming opinion within the CPGB at that time was that Britain was 'on the verge of a revolutionary situation'. An upsurge would sweep away the workers' 'illusions' in Parliament. So to advance the possibility of using Parliament as an instrument of reform was to dupe the proletariat.

However, despite the support of the majority for the Comintern line, the young CPGB could not gain mass support for their strategic perspective. Despite the relative sophistication of the Comintern's synthesis of mass struggle with the utilisation of legal 'auxiliary centres' such as Parliament, the idea of Leninist insurrection did not go down well. In fact it made things very difficult for the British Party, especially on the question of its objective to affiliate to the Labour Party.

In a rather blunt letter dated 10 August 1920 the provisional executive of the CPGB applied to the Labour Party for affiliation. The letter was neither conciliatory nor carefully designed to achieve its tactical objective. It declared that the

CPGB supported the Soviet system of government 'as a means whereby the working class shall achieve power and take control of the forces of production'. It pronounced in favour of 'the dictatorship of the proletariat as a necessary means for combatting the counter-revolution during the transition period between capitalism and communism'. It rejected the view that 'a social revolution can be achieved by the ordinary methods of parliamentary democracy' or by parliamentary action except 'as providing a means of propaganda and agitation towards the revolution'. The CPGB parliamentary representatives must hold a mandate from the Communist Party and not from the particular constituency for which they happened to sit. Quite clearly, despite their bluntness, these points were a crude distillation of the ideas also found in the theses on parliamentariansim adopted by the Comintern. But their fidelity to the spirit of Leninist communism undermined the Leninist objective of affiliation.

One month later, Arthur Henderson, on behalf of the Executive of the Labour Party, rejected the application on the grounds that the objects of the Communist Party 'did not appear to be in accordance with the constitution, programme and principles of the Labour Party'. *(Labour Party Annual Conference Report, 1921,* pp.19-20). The likelihood of such a response should have been obvious to the leaders of the CPGB when they drafted the letter. Their intransigence stemmed from a naive moralistic desire to assert their revolutionary purity, or from a desire to appease the anti-affiliation wing of the Party and those potential recruits also opposed to affiliation.

There is no doubt that a major factor in determining the lack of success of the repeated efforts of the CPGB to affiliate to the Labour Party was the expressed Communist desire to break up the system of parliamentary democracy in a proletarian insurrection, whilst in the meantime using Parliament as a rostrum only. The catastrophist economic perspectives of the early Comintern also meant that the CPGB just wrote off attempts to gain reforms for the workers through Parliament as bound to fail from the outset. Such attitudes were anathema to most trade unionists and individual members of the Labour Party. There may have been widespread support for the Russian Revolution but that was seen, in the main, as a revolt against Tsarist autocracy in a country with quite different conditions to those in Britain.

Most workers could not be convinced that economic reforms, and structural reforms of Parliament itself, were not possible. After all, legislation in 1918, by extending the franchise for men, and giving women the vote for the first time, had increased the electorate from 30 to 74 per cent of the adult population. The Labour Party was growing rapidly in membership and support, so the prospect of a Labour Government was preferred to the dubious experience of insurrection, civil war, and 'dictatorship'.

### *The Communist Party in Parliament*

In the General Election of 1922 the Labour Party put up 411 candidates, a higher number than ever before, but leaving 204 seats without a Labour candidate. It was the policy of the CPGB until 1924 not to put up candidates against a contestant from the Labour Party, but given the lack of blanket coverage by Labour it was possible for the CPGB to field 5 candidates. Most of them had the support of local members of the Labour Party, and one member of the CPGB, S. Saklatvala, stood as an official Labour Party candidate. He, and one other Communist, J.W. Newbold, were elected to Parliament. Saklatvala accepted the Labour Whip. Newbold applied for it, but was rejected. They were both frequent speakers in Parliament, against unemployment and British imperialist policy overseas. Newbold was suspenaed from the House in May 1923 for disobeying the Speaker. (See James Klugmann, *History of the CPGB*, vol.1, pp.192-3).

It did not seem that full advantage was taken by the Communist Party as a whole of this fervent vocal representation in Parliament. In fact, Klugmann, in his rarely-critical 'official' history of the CPGB wrote in the 1960s on the attitude of Party members to their elected representatives in the 1920s:

> 'it could not be said that all members of the Party were convinced of the importance of such work. And of those who, on the surface, *were* convinced, *some* still saw such participation as a purely *negative* act, i.e. they saw only a potential platform from which reaction could be exposed and general Marxist principles enunciated, but not at all clearly the positive way in which the struggle on immediate issues in Council or Parliament could aid and complement the mass struggle outside. Nor did they see how the *combined* struggle, inside and outside, *could*

win concrete gains for the working class even within the framework of capitalism . . . ' (Ibid., p.195).

However, what Klugmann does not make clear is that this 'negative' attitude was part of the official policy of the Communist International and therefore binding on all members of the CPGB. What could be more 'negative' than this thesis passed by the Second Comintern Congress:

> 'This activity inside parliament . . . consists chiefly in revolutionary agitation from the parliamentary tribune, in exposing enemies, in the ideological mobilisation of the masses . . . ' (Degras, op.cit., p.153).

The Third Comintern Congress, meeting in July 1921, rejected the possibility of winning 'concrete gains within the framework of capitalism'. The working class

> 'demands an improvement in its lot, which is at present absolutely incompatible with the objective possibilities of capitalism'. (Ibid., p.237).

The catastrophist perspective of the Comintern muted and serious struggle for reforms within the framework of capitalism. Most members of the CPGB were imbued with this spirit. No wonder they saw Parliament as no more than a propagandist rostrum.

### *The Experience of the First Labour Government*

The Communist Party put up 9 candidates in the General Election of December 1923. Only 2 were standing directly for the CPGB, the remainder stood with either official Labour endorsement or local Labour support. None of the candidates were put up against official Labour candidates. Not one Communist got elected.

The Labour vote increased massively, and in the new year a minority Labour Government was formed. The CPGB did not object to the Labour Party accepting the mantle of office, but they insisted that they should govern only on a socialist programme, and go to the country again if thwarted in Parliament. A joint statement by the leaderships of both the Comintern and the CPGB, issued in February 1924, declared support for the Government insofar as it improved the 'position of the working class' and reduced the danger of war. The Comintern made its attitude clear in the following resolution:

> 'If (we do not expect it) it should become possible to drive the Labour Government by proletarian class movements into a fight with capitalism, the internal crisis in England would thereby be rendered extremely acute. But if, as is to be expected, the Labour Government betrays the interests of the proletariat, it will thus offer the best possible object lesson to the proletariat, enabling it to free itself from the illusions of capitalist democracy, and will thereby accelerate the revolutionising of the working class'. (Quoted in H. Dewar, *Communist Politics in Britain,* p.43).

This was the Leninist principle of supporting Labour 'as a rope supports a hanged man'. However, ironically, the Tories and Liberals were tolerating the Labour Government for the same reason – to 'expose' it.

The formation of the first Labour Government raised working-class aspirations and encouraged a wave of industrial militancy. Within a few months workers came out on strike on tha railways, dockyards, building sites, and London transport system. These groups of workers were opposed by the Labour Government but energetically supported by the Communist Party. By April 1924, the leadership of the CPGB had come to the following assessment:

> 'In every direction the Labour Government has shown itself the servant of the bourgeoisie . . . it is more than ever necessary that in all sections of the working class movement a strong and united effort should be made to compel them to operate their own promises and pledges'. (*Workers' Weekly*, 25 April 1924).

Despite the Labour Government having 'shown itself' as an opponent of the working class, members did not flock to the Communist Party. Its membership did not increase above 4000.

The 1924 Labour Party Conference again discussed CPGB affiliation to the Labour Party. The old issues of dictatorship and parliamentary democracy came to the fore. The Executive Committee recommended rejection of affiliation, stating that the Labour Party

> 'seeks to achieve the Socialist Commonwealth by means of Parliamentary Democracy . . . the Communist Party seeks to achieve the "dictatorship of the proletariat" by armed insurrection'. (*1924 Conference Report,* p.20).

Not only was affiliation rejected by a large majority

but also the conference resolved to bar CPGB members from standing as Labour Party candidates in elections.

As if to confirm the intention of 'armed insurrection' the CPGB paper *Workers' Weekly* published an open letter to the armed forces on 25 July 1924 calling upon the 'workers in uniform' to 'organise passive resistance' and summoned them to 'Turn your weapons on your oppressors!' This out-of-the-blue appeal was directed to a professional rather than a conscript army, in a period of Labour Government for which the CPGB had pledged 'support'. It played an indirect but instrumental role in bringing down the Labour Government. A leader of the CPGB was arrested for sedition. Communists, left-wingers, and Labour backbenchers protested vigorously. The prosecution was dropped. The Tories in Parliament then charged the Government as being subject to extremist pressure. The Liberals combined with them to bring down the Labour Government.

A general election followed in October 1924. The Communists argued for a new Labour Government that would fight for the working class. They put up 8 candidates, one against an official Labour candidate. Most of the rest had Labour Party support in the localities. Just one, Saklatvala, now directly a CPGB candidate but still with the support of the local Labour Party, was elected. The total vote of the 8 candidates came to 55,345. This represented a fall in votes per candidate over 1923. The Labour Party, however, increased its vote massively, from 4.4 million to 5.5 million. Despite the decidely non-radical nature of the Labour Government of 1924 the Labour Party attracted a large increase in its support. The working class, once again, did not flock to the Communist Party, despite the 'exposure' of the Labour leaders. However, despite the increase in the Labour vote, the British electoral system rewarded the Tories with an overall majority in Parliament. The onset of a Tory administration shifted the emphasis of rank-and-file working class struggle more to the industrial field, where the CPGB was beginning to feel more and more at home. For the average CPGB member an economistic and quasi-syndicalist practice began to mask the nagging reality of the continuing allegiance of the British working class to 'capitalist democracy'.

### *The General Strike*

This is not the place to give an account of the nine day General Strike that ended in betrayal. However, we must agree with James Hinton and Richard Hyman, in their book *Trades Unions and Revolution,* when they argue that a revolutionary situation did not develop. The consciousness and organisation of the working class was not sufficiently advanced, and the ruling class was not sufficiently weakened.

What we wish to examine is the political position taken by the Communist Party, particularly in relation to the question of government. In the localities the Communists worked to strengthen and support the strike. Mainly under local Labour Party and trade union instigation many 'Councils of Action' sprung up throughout the country at the onset of the strike. Although the CPGB worked hard to build these Councils they were not treated as incipient Soviets. This attitude was realistic, for the Councils did not match Soviets in cohesion or social prominence. They were forums to discuss specific defensive actions during the strike, linking up local trade union and Labour leaders in their *existing* organisations. The mass of the working class saw the strike as one over wages, not over political or state power. Quite correctly, therefore, Hinton and Hyman come to the conclusion:

> 'There is good reason to believe that, had the CP attempted to politicize the struggle by raising the demand "All power to the Councils of Action", the slogan would have fallen even flatter than did its demand for nationalization of the mines and a General Election'. (p.44).

The situation, it seems, was not near one of 'dual power'.

What, in fact, was the position of the CPGB during the strike? Four slogans were given prominence in the first issue of the *Workers' Bulletin,* the duplicated Communist paper:

> 'Not a penny off the pay, not a second on the day;
> a council of action in every town;
> make friends with the soldiers;
> every man behind the miners'.

The second issue, two days later on 5 May, the third day of the strike, contained a Party pronouncement on 'The Political Meaning of the Strike'. More key slogans emerged:

> 'Nationalization of the mines, without compensation for the coal owners, under workers' control through pit committees!'
> 'Resignation of the Forgery Government! Formation of a Labour Government!'

The latter was an obvious reference to the forgery of the Zinoviev letter, which was used to undermine support for the Labour Government just before the General Election of 1924. The implication must be that if it were not for that forgery Labour would still be in power, and clearly the CPGB at the time would have preferred that state of affairs. Given the relationship of forces, and the absence of a revolutionary situation, any realistic attempt to politicize the struggle forced the CPGB to advance the call for a Labour Government. The simple reason was that there was no existing alternative. The Councils of Action were not in a position to overthrow the capitalist state, so the most preferable situation was a party in Parliament most ready to favour the workers. The CPGB was far too small – so it must be the Labour Party. The logic was relentless.

The above position taken by the CPGB cannot be explained by the then links between the Trades Union Congress and the Soviet Government. It is more likely that the CPGB was reaching a realistic prognosis of the actual situation, and drawing the appropriate conclusions. But in doing so it once more questioned the reason for its own existence. It could be no more than the militant stiffening of the rank-and-file; it was forced to evacuate the governmental sphere and leave that to the Labour Party.

### *The 'Third Period'*

By the General Election of 1929 a number of changes had taken place both within and outside the Communist Party. As a result of the decision of the Liverpool Conference of the Labour Party in 1925, and after some struggle within the Labour Party against that decision, Communists could no longer be individual members of the Labour Party. Both in the CPGB, and the Comintern as a whole, the ultra-left 'New Line' of the so-called 'Third Period' was in operation. All social-democratic parties, including the Labour Party, were vigorously denounced as 'social fascist'. The slogan of support for a Labour Government was not to be found, and instead there was a call for a 'Revolutionary Workers' Government'. Where Communist candidates were not standing in elections the British worker was asked to abstain. Harry Pollitt and Palme Dutt had been installed as the new leadership of the CPGB.

The Communist Party entered the electoral fray with its own independent banner. It put up 25 candidates, more than trebling their 1924 effort. The result was a disaster. Not one Communist was elected, and they lost their single representative in Parliament. The aggregate vote of the Party fell, despite the increase in the number of candidates, to 50,614. In 1924 the average vote for every Communist candidate was 25 per cent. In 1929 it was 5.3 per cent.

With another big increase in the Labour vote the Second Labour Government was formed. The CPGB attitude to the Government was sectarian and uncomprimising. In January 1930 Communists were told in the *Communist Review* that the tasks of the Party were

> 'to place itself at the head of the rising wave of struggle. . . . To assist the workers to break through the shackles of the bureaucratic machine by effective revolutionary leadership . . . While the sum of all this is the fight for the overthrow of the Labour Government'.

This was practically a call to instant insurrection.

In fact, one man did 'overthrow' the Labour Government – the Labour Prime Minister Ramsay MacDonald. He deserted the Labour Party to form a National Government with the Conservatives and Liberals. Two months later a General Election was called. In the 1931 election the line of the CPGB was more or less the same as in 1929. However, due to the gravity of MacDonald's betrayal and widespread disgust in the Labour movement, the Communist Party attracted more votes. With 26 candidates their aggregate vote was 74,824. But no Communist got elected to Parliament. The percentage vote per CPGB candidate was 7.5.

In January 1933 Hitler stormed to power in Germany. Fascism was clearly on the march in Europe. The attention of the Labour movement was directed to issues of international politics, as well as to the domestic arena. At the same time the prestige of the CPGB became more and more connected with the international standing of the Soviet Union. And that was clearly on the rise, as the USSR was seen as the main bulwark against the fascist threat.

However, even after Hitler's victory the 'Third Period' line still continued for a while. Pollitt, General Secretary of the CPGB, argued that the rise of fascism was destroying 'illusions' about parliamentary democracy, and

> 'In this way an important weakening of Social Democracy takes place, which, because it is the chief social support of capitalism, leads to a strengthening of the revolutionary forces making for the overthrow of capitalism'. (Quoted in H. Dewar, op.cit., p.104).

*The Popular Front*

Eventually, through the direction of the Comintern, the policy of the Communist movement changed. Communists were told that 'the situation had changed', not that the previous policy had been in error. The policy was now to seek unity with socialist, social-democratic, democratic and pacifist organisations in a common front against fascism. The CPGB did an about-turn. In October 1935 the Party dropped its often-pronounced slogan 'For Soviet Britain' and called 'For a Labour Government'. At various times during the 1920s the Party had advanced *both* such slogans, so there was a double significance to this move. First, it was an adaptation to the parliamentary *status quo* and an implicit partial renunciation of Leninism. Second, it was a gesture of support for Labour after 6 years of extreme acrimony and sectarianism, during which the Labour Party had been described as 'social fascist'.

As a further gesture of conciliation the CPGB

fielded only 2 candidates in November 1935, campaigning elsewhere for the Labour Party. Despite the fact that CPGB candidates were both opposed by Labour candidates one, Gallacher, did get elected to Parliament. The CPGB candidates got an average of 38.0 per cent. It seemed that the threat of fascism had driven many people into the newly-opened arms of the Communists. However, only once more in its existence was the CPGB to get more than an average of 10 per cent of the poll in constituencies where it put up candidates.

Gradually the attitude of the CPGB to parliamentary democracy, in line with the Comintern, began to change. The main objective was now the fight against fascism. Socialist revolution, whilst still being desirable, had to be postponed until after the victory over fascism. This shift in perspective allowed the Party to ignore the insurrectionary objective in its day-to-day practice, act in a manner similar to a normal social-democratic party, but maintain a nominal adherence to Leninism. Nevertheless the slogan of the 'dictatorship of the proletariat' still provided some embarrassment. So the Central Committee of September 1937 explained that the 'dictatorship of the proletariat', although remaining Party doctrine, since it really meant not dictatorship but 'a very broad form of democracy for the working people', was a slogan not to be referred to in future as the Party had to 'make it clear that this issue is not now on the order of the day in the present situation in Britain'. (*Central Committee Report,* 1938, pp.76-7). I am sure that it was all very clear. The 'dictatorship of the proletariat' was Party doctrine, but it was not to be used as a slogan; it said 'dictatorship', but it really meant 'democracy'; it was not the order of the day for the present, so that meant it could not also be used for the future. A stunning example of 'dialectical logic'.

*The Second World War*

The War brought further zig-zags in Party policy. At first, in support of the British Government's stand against the German invasion of Poland, the Party declared its 'readiness to take part in any struggle, political or military, to secure the defeat of fascism'. (*Daily Worker,* 2 September 1939.) But within days, as the implications of the Nazi-Soviet pact became clear, the line had to change. It was in the interests of the USSR, they thought, that the pact made between Hitler and Stalin was to be supported. Slavish submission to the Soviet regime came to dominate shallow expediency and conciliation at home. So, on 7 October, the *Daily Worker* declared: 'This war is not a war for democracy against fascism'. Palme Dutt, in a pamphlet *Why This War* wrote in November that it was British imperialism not German or Italian fascism, that was 'the principal and most aggressive force of world reaction'. This was almost a return to the sort of ultra-leftism of the 'Third Period'.

It was the Nazi attack on the Soviet Union of June 1941 which ended the Hitler-Stalin pact, and allowed a measure of sanity to return to the CPGB. But a 'sane' political party is not necessarily one with the appropriate slogan at the right period of time. A sane person is one in genuine contact with the real world. The only means of contact that a political party has with reality is through a living and critical internal democracy. The ultra-left turn of 1929, the swing to the ultra-left equation of fascism with democracy in 1939, had rid the CPGB of all critical elements who did not willingly accept these zig-zags. Meaningful internal discussion and democracy had long ceased to exist.

The single overriding rationale to Party policy since 1929 was the short-term interests of the Soviet regime. Those that accepted the line must accept those interests above even the objective of socialism in Britain. Through these processes the Party quite simply lost its ability to analyse the situation at home, digest new information, and relate to real social forces. Any corrections or improvements in the Party line for many years after 1941 must be seen in this light.

After 1941 the CPGB rolled up its sleeves and took the Allied side in the war. The war was now one for 'socialism and democracy'. The Party zealously supported the drive for increased war production and the National Government ban on strikes. On demonstrations Communists carried Winston Churchill's portrait side by side with that of Stalin.

### *The 1945 General Election*

Conciliation had gone so far by 1945 that the CPGB was to the right of a large section of the Labour Party. The Communist International had been dissolved in 1943 but the CPGB still carried on with the old policy of making the Soviet regime first political priority. At the General Election the Party did not call for a Labour Government, but intimated its desire for a continuance of the Churchill-led coalition, after the war had ended. The Party put up 21 candidates, obtained an average of 12.7 per cent of the poll, and won two seats. This was the last time that the CPGB obtained representation in Parliament. Labour was returned with an absolute majority for the first time.

The Labour victory took the Communist Party by surprise. The Communists hoped to play a part in an expected post-war coalition, but the Labour majority made such plans obsolete. Furthermore, when the Labour Government managed to carry out some significant reforms, such as the setting up of the National Health Service and the nationalisation of a few key industries, some old political dogmas were challenged, and the situation was made difficult for the CPGB. Their previous view, that major social reforms were impossible under capitalism, was defied by the realities of the post-war capitalist reconstruction.

In the first two decades of its existence the Communist International had preached that major economic reforms were impossible under the present capitalist epoch. In addition, it was argued, this fact was the 'material basis' for the rejection of reformism and parliamentarianism. It was these 'objective conditions' that had rendered Parliament a 'talking shop' and move the 'centre of gravity' of political action away from Parliament. It seemed to follow, therefore, that when capitalism was no longer unable to deliver the goods, and significant reforms were possible, that the old Comintern position became obsolete. If the material basis of anti-parliamentarianism was the stagnation or decline of capitalism, then a capitalist boom would seem to justify a parliamentary road to socialism.

In capitulating to parliamentary reformism, therefore, the leaders of the CPGB were simply carrying out the catastrophist logic of the early Comintern. What was wrong with the latter-day position of the CPGB was the obverse of what was wrong with the policies of the early Comintern. Just as it was wrong to argue that a period of capitalist expansion validated a strategy centred on Parliament, it was also wrong to argue that a period of capitalist stagnation validated a strategy centred outside that institution. In fact, however, a strategy for socialism that is centred mainly on Parliament is bound to fail, whatever the general trajectory of capitalist development. The reasons for its shortcomings are primarily to do with the structures of political power and the nature of the state. They have little to do with the growth rate of the capitalist economy. A socialist transformation is not possible without the creation of mass organs of popular power, as without such instruments of change a socialist majority within Parliament is bound to remain imprisoned within the existing capitalist social formation.

So it was that the economistic analysis of the early Comintern, despite its catastrophist tenor, made the CPGB vulnerable to reformist pressures. It is an irony of history that the most eloquent expositor of the position adopted by the Comitern in its early years was none other than Leon Trotsky.

*The Introduction of the CPGB's Parliamentary Road*

The CPGB was never to admit its inversion of classic Leninist positions. It failed to accept the distance it had travelled since its foundation. The final and complete break from the Leninist conception of an insurrectionary road to socialism came in 1951 with the introduction of the Party document *The British Road to Socialism.* Its strategy was centred on the need to capture a majority of socialist and Communist seats in Parliament. At the time, however, the novelty of this approach was not emphasised. Only 'the situation had changed' and some 'alterations' were necessary. Pollitt went so far as to assert that it was 'slanderous' to suggest that the Party had ever believed in creating soviets in Britain. (*World News,* ii, p.946). The truth was that the Party had continued to advocate the establishment of soviets right up to 1935, and even in that year the official programme of the Party was entitled *For Soviet Britain.* Once again the line of the Party changed in a fundamental way, but the leadership spoke and acted as if everything was basically the same.

The evidence indicates that the discussion of the *British Road to Socialism* was far from rigorous and intensive. Some objectors raised their heads but these either left the Party or were expelled. The Party had little internal democracy and real debate. Its practice and routine was now, in substance, classically reformist, so without any collective thought on the matter it was not difficult to make the change.

Minor amendments were made to the *British Road* by the Party Congresses of 1957 and 1967. but in substance it remained the same. It is more convenient and generous, therefore, to cease all historical narrative and examine the theoretical content of the version published in 1968.

## *The Third Revised Edition of 1968*

The important change of line in *The British Road to Socialism* was justified by an assertion that

> 'socialism is a reality for all to see. Countries with a population of hundreds of millions are socialist states. . . . This new relation of forces in the world opens up new possibilities of winning political power without armed struggle. Such a peaceful, democratic advance to socialism can, in the Communist Party's view, be achieved in Britain if the great majority of the people desire it'. (1968 ed., p.17).

Whilst it was true that vast areas of the world were taken out of the capitalist world market in the 1940s (Eastern Europe and China) the argument for a change of line was unconvincing. First, people had begun to realise the extent of the horrors of Stalin's rule in the 1930s, the rigged trials, purges, and extermination of millions of peasants. The Soviet Union was far from being an unblemished attraction. Second, as unemployment in the developed capitalist countries began to drop, the economic benefits of the Soviet system seemed less significant, and the demerits in terms of lack of civil liberties more profound. Third, even if the Soviet Bloc was in a much stronger ideological, political, and military position in the post-war world the conclusion could not be drawn that the transition to socialism in the West would necessarily be peaceful. Would the capitalists not resist by force even from a weak position? And would the Soviet Bloc come to the assistance of a new revolutionary movement or socialist regime? The failure of Stalin to come to the aid of the Greek Communists in the 1940s hardly suggested that the Soviet Union would energetically defend every new socialist revolution or regime in the West.

Whilst the argumentation for the change of line was, itself, unconvincing, the extent of the change was masked by changing the meaning of some crucial words in the Marxist dictionary. The most important concerns the definition of 'reformism'. People such as Eduard Bernstein were dubbed by Lenin and Luxemburg as reformist because they held that *socialism could gradually replace capitalism* by a series of reforms, passed by a government dominated by a socialist party. However, *The British Road to Socialism* saw reformism as something different:

> 'Reformism – the acceptance of the framework of the capitalist foreign policy, *the renunciation of socialism* – inevitably leads to fiasco'. (p.19, my emphasis – G.H.).

This formulation is no accident. It appears in many Communist Party pamphlets and articles, as recently as March 1977 by Gordon McLennan in

*Marxism Today* (p.70). Not only is this new definition at variance with orthodox Leninism it is an attempt to obscure its own accommodation to classic reformism, and to maintain the impression of papal infallibility. The CPGB creates an enormous amount of confusion and imprecision, both within and outside its own ranks.

### *'By Peaceful Means'*

The key statement of the CPGB strategy for socialist change is on pages 47-54 of the 1968 *British Road.* This is unlike an orthodox Leninist strategy, in that Parliament is seen as the main organ of political power. Neither soviets or workers' councils are advocated. Parliament is not to be 'smashed', nor is it to be treated simply as a 'rostrum'. The central aim is to win a socialist and Communist majority in the House of Commons.

As we have suggested in arguments elsewhere, there are some positive features to this adjustment in strategy. In particular, it is a positive step to advocate the continuance of Parliament, and its use to help achieve real social and economic reforms under both capitalism and socialism, in advanced capitalist democracies such as Britain. But we look in vain in the *British Road* of 1968 for a solid argument to support this position. There is little else other than the spurious statement about the 'new balance of world forces' discussed above. There is no discussion or analysis of the form and function of the structure of state power, nor of the efficacy of the mechanisms of socialist change. The unfortunate impression is created, therefore, that Parliament is now the centre of attraction because it is by far the main instrument of social revolution.

To slightly counter this impression there are a few references to an additionally necessary 'mass movement'. But it is not clear what the actions of this 'mass movement' are to be, nor what institutional forms this movement is to take. Hence there is little to dispel a view that the main role of the 'mass movement' is electoral activity.

This leads on to the question of force. On two occasions the *British Road* discusses the possibility of the ruling class using force to resist socialist change. We quote the relevant passages in full:

> 'The ruling class will not easily surrender wealth and power. On the contrary, it will strive by every means, direct and indirect, constitutional and unconstitutional, to restrain and impede the popular movement, to break its strength or sap its unity. Against all such attempts popular vigilance and mass action will be essential. The working class and popular movement will need to be ready to use its organised strengh to prevent or defeat attempts at violence against it, its organisations or representatives, or illegal actions by reactionary forces at home or by agents of their foreign allies. There will be particular dangers of such resort to force at crucial stages of the struggle, for instance when a general election is likely to result in a socialist majority; or even more when a socialist government has been returned and is taking essential measures to break the economic and political power of the monopolies. The extent to which the popular movement, above all its working class core, is informed and vigilant, the extent to which it is geared to bring all its formidable strength into play in support of socialist policies, will be the decisive factor. This strength

> will determine whether the verdict is accepted, or whether, in defence of their interests, the capitalists resist by force'. (pp.49-50).

The second passage is shorter:

> 'Only against illegal opposition would the force of the law be invoked; only in the case of violence against the socialist government would forceful measures be taken by the state and the people'. (p.51).

It is better that the *British Road* had mentioned the possibility of the use of reactionary force against a socialist government than it had not been mentioned at all. But what is striking about these passages is their vagueness and abstractness. The working class must be 'vigilant', yet we are not told what would be the appropriate signals for which it sould be watchful, not what actions it should carry out in the event of the capitalists using force, nor what organisations are to carry out such activity and vigilance. The 'popular movement' will have to 'bring all its formidable strength into play'. Yet there is no suggestion of the means by which this strength is to be expressed. I expect that the CPGB would go so far as to accept the idea of a general strike or of 'Councils of Action'. But would they accept armed workers' militias, or insurrection? The latter would be inconsistent with the rest of the *British Road.* The fact that the *British Road* does not mention any concrete expression of working class 'vigilance' means that it is fundamentally weak on this question of force, despite the passages which raise the possibility of resistance by the capitalists. It is one thing to raise the possibility of a danger, it is more important to outline the concrete means of avoiding it.

If the *British Road* had made it clear that in politics questions of social change resolve ultimately to questions of force then two advantages could have been gained. First, illusions in the exclusive power of Parliament would have been undermined. But second, paradoxically, the necessity of gaining a parliamentary majority in an advanced capitalist democracy would have been underlined. For Parliament has a capacity to mobilise social forces, to a degree. If it is in the hands of socialists it can *aid* a military struggle against reactionaries; if it is in the hands of reactionaries it is a formidable weapon *against* any militant socialist movement.

### *Democracy and the State*

The endemic vagueness of the *British Road* spreads to other key issues. The word 'socialism' is never defined clearly, and the impression is often given that it simply means a nationalised economy. The structures of power under socialism are discussed in the following way:

> 'A socialist government requires a socialist state machine. Without this political power of the people, expressed in the democratic decision of the electoral majority, cannot be effective nor can socialism be built. The leading positions in the Ministries and departments, the armed forces and the police, the nationalised industries and other authorities must, therefore, be filled by men and women loyal to socialism and with experience of the problems and way of life of the people. This ensures that the socialist policies determined on by Parliament are

> fully implemented. The aim is to make the socialist state machinery the servant of the people and their needs'. (p.53).

Other than what is implied in the above passage it is never made clear what a 'socialist state machine' means. Does it mean the 'political power of the people, expressed in the democratic decision of the electoral majority'? But that is consistent with merely representative parliamentary government, within a capitalist state. It is implied that it is merely a question of replacing individuals in 'leading positions' in the civil service and nationalised industries. The naive faith is expressed that as these individuals would be 'loyal to socialism' then that would be sufficient to ensure that the state machinery served the people. This is idealist and un-Marxist. Although the outlook and convictions of individuals in power are important it is also necessary to look at the social and institutional forces which can lead such people astray. The history of the socialist movement is littered with cases of individuals whose socialist convictions were disarmed by social pressures, or by their own isolation from a mass socialist movement. The character of a state machine is not determined by the convictions of the individuals within it, but by its relation to social forces, its connections with the social relations of production, and its own internal structures.

Under capitalism the masses are denied significant political power because of the inegalitarian structures of political and economic control. This denial is reinforced in a whole series of ways.

Without fundamental changes in political structures and socio-economic relations the masses will still be excluded from popular and extensive democratic control. Hence the insertion of socialist individuals into key positions of power will not break down the barriers which exclude the masses from effective control of their social and economic environment.

The task of building a network of mass institutions of working class power, to complement a reformed Parliament, is closely connected to the question of resisting any armed force that may be used by the capitalist class against the socialist movement. In modern conditions such reactionary force can only be resisted or defeated by the activities and appeals of a mass popular movement, organised in, or closely related to, mass democratic institutions in the localities. Thus institutions such as Councils of Action play a dual role: first as democratic organs of working class power, and second, as instruments to organise resistance to reactionary force.

The failure of the *British Road* to deal with these material and institutional questions is symptomatic. The actual detachment of the Party from institutional reality is reflected in its programme. The Party thus relapses into the practice of seeing politics merely as a contest of ideas. Its role then becomes one of a mere purveyor of ideology, its aim being one of 'raising the consciousness of the working class' simply through the passage of correct ideas into the heads of the masses. The necessary material and institutional basis for such a process of 'consciousness raising' is neglected.

## *Between the Idea and the Reality*

There are two main explanations for these weaknesses. First, the Communist Party was prevented from advocating organisations of mass popular power by its traditional submission to the Soviet regime. Support for meaningful and extensive democratic institutions would be an implied criticism of the Soviet Union, where no such institutions exist However, whilst remaining a cause up to the present day, the fragmentation of the Communist world and the invasion of Czechoslovakia have undermined the importance of this particular inhibition. A second reason for the weaknesses has existed since the 1920s, and is becoming relatively more important. It is rooted in the structures and practice of the CPGB itself. It is not just the failure to analyse fully the structures of economic, social and political power in post-war Britain, although that is important. It is not just the lack of sufficient inner-Party democracy, although that is essential. It is the conception, tradition and practice of endowing the leadership of the Party and the Party itself with the God-like capacity of determining the total political truth of a situation, thus denying the 'epistemological' role of a two-way dialogue within the Party, between the Party and the working class, and denying the need for Party structures and practices which embody a living relationship with real social forces. The programme of the Party becomes founded on vague abstractions, not real social and economic conditions and movements. Its power becomes one of moral imperative or fatalist belief in the 'growing progressive movement' and ultimate victory to come. It adopts the idealist practice of seeing its own ideas as the engine of its own success, instead of the materialist practice of using real social forces as both determinants and bearers of programmatic ideas.

The historical explanation for this aberration is not difficult, and has been touched upon already. The ultra-left turn in the late 1920s detached the CPGB from contact with living reality, and imposed the vacillations of the Moscow line. Given its subservience to the zig-zags of the Comintern a two-way investigative dialogue both within the Party, and between Party and masses, was rendered impossible. The Party became a puppet, suspended from Moscow, and without feet on the stage of British conditions. When the Comintern was dissolved only a link of allegiance remained with the Soviet Union, and this very gradually diminished over time. But the Party remained suspended in a void. It had virtually lost the capacity to think, to evaluate its theory in the light of practice. It resorted to panacea and abstraction.

In *Tribune* of 22 April 1977, Jimmy Reid gave some illustrative examples of the failure of the CPGB to come to grips with reality. He describes a cartoon which appeared in the *Morning Star* a few weeks earlier, and which suggests that Prime Minister Callaghan could and should form an alliance with the Communist Party to overcome Labour's electoral difficulties, just as Socialists and Communists formed an alliance in France. As Reid put it: 'The unreality is breathtaking'. The enormous difference between the sizes of the French and British Communist Parties is not considered. In Britain the Labour Party gets a vote six-hundred times greater than the Communist Party. The CPGB have not managed to get an MP in Parliament since 1945. The reality is that, in electoral terms, the CPGB has nothing to offer the Labour Party. This is the reality the CPGB refuses to face.

*Recent Developments*

A new draft of *The British Road to Socialism* appeared in 1977. In many ways it is an improvement on previous versions. It has a more adequate social and economic analysis of British capitalism. It discusses some of the forces of social change in more detail. It recognises the heterogeneity of the Labour movement and includes, for the first time, support for the Women's Liberation Movement. It repeats the declaration, in a slightly more forceful manner, of the need to resist right wing force against a left government. But on the whole it is much the same as the previous versions. More significantly, it indicates no change in the structures and practice of the CPGB.

First, what is the justification for the new programme? The answer is found on the first page:

> 'there have been big changes in Britain and the world'.

There have, indeed, been big changes. But is it not also possible that the previous programmes had some deficiencies as well? Or was the programme of 1968 completely adequate for 1968? As we have seen, every change in the line of the CPGB since 1920 has been justified not by an admission of past mistakes but by an appeal to a supposedly 'changed situation'. A myth of Party infallibility is perpetuated. Evaluation of past mistakes, self-education from past experiences, are ruled out. The membership of the Party is not allowed to learn from the errors of the past, it is simply expected to ratify the broad outline of the programme.

Full democracy is impossible without constructive criticism and self-criticism. Yet there is very little material in the new *British Road to Socialism* which is critical of the Communist Party. There is no serious examination of its functioning, structures, and performance. Yet there is frequent and eager criticism of the Labour Party and Labour Governments. (Which is not to say that there is not plenty of scope for criticism here). It is noted that the Labour vote has fallen by 10 percentage points since 1951, falling to its previous level of 1935. The fall is attributed to the old reformist strategies of Labour Governments. But, as Reid points out, appropriate criticisms of Labour are not matched by even a glance at the electoral performance of the Communist Party. Neither the decline in the Communist vote, nor the decline in the membership of the Party, are even mentioned in the new programme. If a 10 per cent fall in the Labour vote since 1951 is attributed to 'bad policies', then to what do we attribute a fall in the average Communist vote per candidate from 38 per cent in 1935 to 4 per cent in 1951, and a further fall to 1.5 per cent in October 1974? Again there is a complete refuse to face reality, and even start the process of drawing appropriate conclusions.

## *The Political Character of the 'British Road'*

The lack of Communist self-criticism in the *British Road* is symptomatic of the failure to engage the programme with real social forces, and take account of the unfavourable progress of the CPGB. Allegiance to the strategy of the *British Road* by the members of the CPGB has become like a ritual, with little real meaning in the day-to-day practice of the membership. Today the Party is little else than a network of contacts for militant trade unionists, plus a forum for the discussion and development of Marxist theory. These activities and functions are positive and useful, but they are not sufficient to constitute the CPGB as an intervening, thinking, revolutionary party. The CPGB is reaping the harvest of its own history: the zigzags of the past, and the failure of successive Party leaderships to argue their politics and convince the membership *politically*, other than by crude organisational manoeuvre.

The politics of the Party are simply unconvincing to the outsider, partly because of their abstractness and partly because the Party has not won the trust of the Labour movement. The Party wishes to preserve Parliament, so why does it still call itself Leninist? The Party accepts the need for an institutionalised opposition under socialism, so why does it not allow formal opposition within its own ranks? The list of contradictions is endless.

Behind all these faults is a deep malaise. The lack of trust, internal democracy and proper political discussion are its symptoms. The disease is an incapacity to relate the strategy of the Party to any movement or organisation outside the CPGB which displays its own autonony and initiative. This explains, in particular, the failure to deal with future mass organs of popular power, such as workers' councils, in *The British Road to Socialism,* and the failure to relate concretely to the present mass-based institutions and agencies of socialist change.

It is true that the *British Road* sees extra-parliamentary mass struggle as essential. But the failure to give this concrete and institutional substance means that the balance between parliamentary and extra-parliamentary action shifts excessively towards the parliamentary and electoral sphere. For this reason, in our view, the *British Road* is closer to classic reformism than revolutionary Marxism. We define reformism not in the manner of the CPGB but in its usual, classic, sense. Reformism is a strategy which sees Parliament as the main or exclusive focus for socialist change. In effect the adoption of such a strategy means the separation of the governing socialist elite from a mass movement which displays its own autonomy and initiative. Unless the *British Road* is altered to give the mass struggle both autonomy and concrete institutional content then the application of its strategy in practice will be little else but reformism. A strategy is not judged simply by the form of words that it adopts. It must be related to the context of its practice. Despite the qualifications, the *British Road* when applied in practice will be indistinguishable from the reformism of Bernstein or Kautsky.

It is now easy to see why the crisis within the Communist Party runs so deep. It has lost much of its *raison d'être.* It wears Leninist clothes but embraces classic reformism. It eagerly tries to distance itself from the Labour Party, but offers little alternative to the Labour Party even in its present form. The more it tries to democratise and open up its internal discussion the more it fractures and fragments in the process. It is the sad tale of an organisation deeply scarred by its own history. The Party was founded on Leninist and revolutionary lines: now it is neither. If the Party turns to the necessary problem of its Parliamentary representation then it is forced to face its own abysmal electoral record, and the fact that it will be very unlikely if a Communist ever gets elected to Parliament under the present electoral system. It is far easier for the biblical camel to pass through the eye of a needle than for a member of the Communist Party to enter the British Parliament.

The crisis within the CPGB is a clash of its history and practice with the exigencies of reality. To face this reality means to face the fact that there is little reason for its continued existence as a Party. Politically it has travelled a long way since its first application for Labour Party affiliation in 1920. It has shifted its position on the very issues which were used by the Labour Party leadership of that time to reject that application. It has come to terms with the weight and significance of parliamentary democracy in Western Europe, albeit in an inadequate and somewhat unclear fashion. Tragically, however, it has thus removed its own reasons for its foundation.

# Appendix A

## THE ELECTORAL PERFORMANCE OF THE COMMUNIST PARTY

Note: Statistics for the General Elections of 1922, 1923 and 1924 are not included because in only one constituency, in one of those three elections, was a CPGB candidate opposed by Labour.

| General Election Date | CPGB Membership | CPGB Candidates | CPGB MPs Elected | Total CPGB Vote | Average CPGB percent vote per Candidate | Average Labour percent vote per Candidate |
|---|---|---|---|---|---|---|
| 1929 | 3,500 | 25 | 0 | 50,614 | 5.3 | 39.3 |
| 1931 | 6,279 | 26 | 0 | 74,824 | 7.5 | 33.0 |
| 1935 | 7,700 | 2 | 1 | 27,117 | 38.0 | 40.3 |
| 1945 | 45,435 | 21 | 2 | 102,780 | 12.7 | 50.4 |
| 1950 | 38,853 | 100 | 0 | 91,746 | 2.0 | 46.7 |
| 1951 | | 10 | 0 | 21,640 | 4.4 | 49.2 |
| 1955 | 32,681 | 17 | 0 | 33,144 | 4.2 | 47.3 |
| 1959 | 25,313 | 18 | 0 | 30,897 | 4.1 | 44.5 |
| 1964 | 34,281 | 36 | 0 | 45,932 | 3.4 | 44.1 |
| 1966 | 32,243 | 57 | 0 | 62,112 | 3.0 | 48.7 |
| 1970 | 29,356 | 58 | 0 | 37,970 | 1.1 | 43.5 |
| 1974 (F) | 29,943 | 44 | 0 | 32,741 | 1.7 | 38.0 |
| 1974 (O) | | 29 | 0 | 17,426 | 1.5 | 40.2 |

Sources: H. Pelling, *The British Communist Party*, D. Butler and A. Sloman, *British Political Facts 1900-1975*.

# Appendix B

## DIAGRAMMATIC REPRESENTATION OF VARIOUS SOCIALIST POSITIONS ON PARLIAMENT

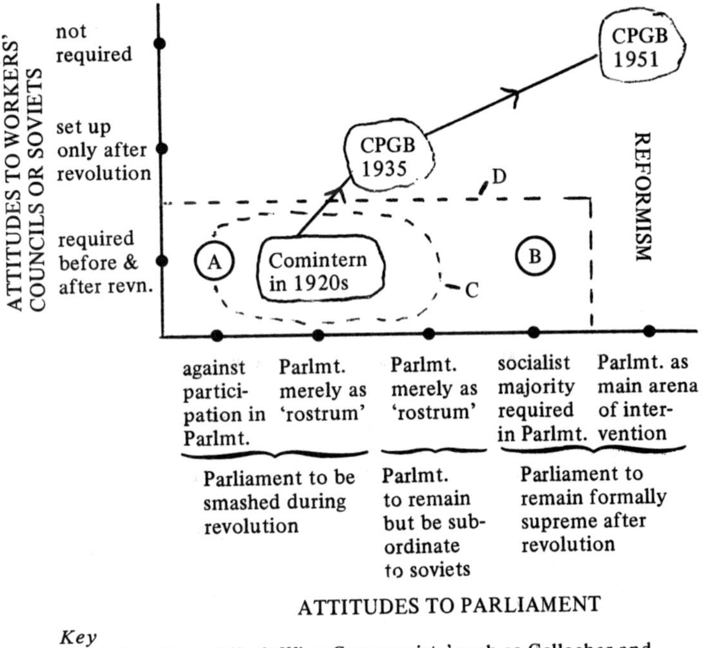


*Key*

A. Position of 'Left-Wing Communists' such as Gallacher and Pankhurst in 1920, and of some far-left groups today.

B. The political position advocated in this book for advanced capitalist democracies.

C. The boundaries of the present-day Trotskyist movement.

D. The boundaries of revolutionary strategy.

# Bibliography

Ali, T., *The Coming British Revolution*, Jonathan Cape, 1972.
Anderson, P., *Passages from Antiquity to Feudalism*, NLB, 1974.
Anderson, P., *Lineages of the Absolute State*, NLB, 1974.
Anderson, P., *Considerations on Western Marxism*, NLB, 1976.
Anderson, P., 'The Antinomies of Antonio Gramsci', *New Left Review* 100, November 1976-January 1977, pp.5-78.
Anderson, P. and Blackburn, R. (eds.), *Towards Socialism*, Collins 1966.
Attlee, C., *The Labour Party in Perspective*, Left Book Club, 1937.
Avineri, S., *The Social and Political Thought of Karl Marx*, Cambridge University Press, 1968.
Benn, A.W., 'A Plea to Labour for Tolerance', *The Guardian*, 13 December 1976.
Blackburn, R., 'What is the "Democratic Road" to Socialism?', *International*, Vol.3, No.4, Summer 1977, pp.18-24.
Butler, D. and Sloman, A., *British Political Facts 1900-75*, Macmillan, 1975.
Cannon, J. and Munis, G., *What Policy for Revolutionists – Marxism or Ultra-Leftism?*, Merit, 1969.
Claudin, F., *The Communist Movement: From Comintern to Cominform*, Peregrene, 1975.
Coates, K., *Beyond Wage Slavery*, Spokesman, 1977.
Coates, K., *Socialists and the Labour Party*, Spokesman Pamphlet, 1975.
Coates, K. (ed.), *The New Worker Co-operatives*, Spokesman, 1976.
Cole, G.D.H., *History of the Labour Party From 1914*, Allen and Unwin, 1948.
Cole, G.D.H., The Meaning of Marxism, Ann Arbor, 1964.
Colletti, L., *From Rousseau to Lenin*, NLB, 1972.
Colletti, L., 'Which Road?', *International*, Vol.2, No.3, Summer 1974, pp.5-6.
Colletti, L., 'Introduction' to Marx *Early Writings*, Pelican 1975.
Communist Party of Great Britain, *The British Road to Socialism*, editions of 1951, 1958, 1968 and 1977 (draft).
Communist Party of Great Britain, *The Communist Unity Convention, Official Report*, facsimile reproduction 1968.

Cripps, S., *Can Socialism Come by Constitutional Means?*, London, n.d.

Degras, J. (ed.), The Communist International, Vols. 1-3, Frank Cass, 1971.

Deutscher, I., *The Prophet Armed,* New York, 1954.

Dewar, H., *Communist Politics in Britain,* Pluto, 1976.

Evans, L. (ed.), *Revolt in France: A Contemporary Record,* Merit, 1968.

Farman, C., *The General Strike,* Panther, 1974.

Fischer, R.M., *Stalin and German Communism,* London, 1948.

Geras, N., *The Legacy of Rosa Luxemburg,* NLB, 1976.

Glucksmann, A., 'Strategy and Revolution in France 1968', *New Left Review* 52, November-December 1968, pp.67-121.

Gorz, A., 'The Way Forward', *New Left Review* 52, November-December 1968, pp.47-66.

Gorz, A., *Socialism and Revolution,* Allen Lane, 1975.

Gramsci, A., *Selections from the Prison Notebooks,* Lawrence and Wishart, 1971.

Habermas, J., *Legitimation Crisis,* Heinemann, 1976.

Hinton, J. and Hyman, R., *Trades Unions and Revolution,* Pluto, 1975.

Hodgson, G., *Trotsky and Fatalistic Marxism,* Spokesman, 1975.

Holland, S., *Strategy for Socialism,* Spokesman, 1975.

Holland, S., *The Socialist Challenge,* Quartet, 1975.

Holland, S., 'The Sell-Out of the Labour Government and the Future of the Left', *Labour Leader,* May 1977.

Hunt, R.N., *The Political Ideas of Marx and Engels,* Vol.1, Macmillan, 1975.

Jenkins, P., 'The Labour Party and the Politics of Transition', *Socialist Register 1977,* Merlin.

Jenkins, R., *Pursuit of Progress,* London 1953.

Jones, G.S., 'The Marxism of the Early Lukacs', *New Left Review* 70, November-December 1971, pp.27-64.

Kautsky, K., *The Dictatorship of the Proletariat,* Ann Arbor, 1964.

Klugmann, J., *History of the Communist Party of Great Britain,* Vols.1-2, Lawrence and Wishart, 1968-9.

Laski, H., *The Crisis and the Constitution,* London, 1932.

Laski, H., *The Secret Battalion,* London, 1946.

Lenin, V.I., *The State and Revolution.*

Lenin, V.I., *The Proletarian Revolution and the Renegade Kautsky.*

Lenin, V.I., *Left-wing Communism – An Infantile Disorder.*

Luxemburg, R. *Reform or Revolution.*

Magri, L., 'The May Events and Revolution in the West', *Socialist Register* 1969, pp.29-54.

Mandel, E., 'Lessons of May', *New Left Review* 52, November-December 1968, pp.9-31,

Mandel, E., 'Shirley Williams on the Road to Samara', *Red Weekly,* 10 February 1977.

Miliband, R., *Parliamentary Democracy*, Merlin, 1973.
Miliband, R., *The State in Capitalist Society*, Quartet, 1973.
Miliband, R., 'Lenin's "The State and Revolution"', *Socialist Register 1970*, Merlin, pp.309-19.
Miliband, R., 'The Coup in Chile', *Socialist Register 1973*, Merlin, pp.451-74.
Mishark, J.W., *The Road to Revolution*, Detroit, 1967.
Moore Jr., B., *Social Origins of Dictatorship and Democracy*, Allen Lane, 1967.
Marx, K., *Early Writings*, Pelican, 1975.
Marx, K., *The Revolution of 1848*, Pelican, 1973.
Marx, K., *Surveys from Exile*, Pelican, 1973.
Marx, K., *The First International and After*, Pelican, 1974.
Marx, K., and Engels, F., *Selected Correspondence*, Moscow, n.d.
Murphy, R.T., *Preparing for Power*, Pluto, 1972.
Pelling, H., *The British Communist Party*, Macmillan, 1968.
Purdy, D., Review Article in *Capital and Class*, No.1, Spring 1977, pp.117-21.
Reid, J., *Reflections of a Clyde Built Man*, Souvenir, 1976.
Reid, J., 'Which is the British Road to Socialism?', *Tribune*, 22 and 29 April 1977.
Roberts, G., 'The Politics of the International Marxist Group', *Marxism Today*, February 1976, pp.46-53.
Roberts, G., 'The Strategy of Rank and Filism', *Marxism Today*, December 1976, pp.375-83.
Roberts, G., 'The CP, the SWP and the Strategy for Socialism in Britain', *International Socialism*, No.99, June 1977, pp.22-4.
Roberts, G., 'Trotskyism and Revolution', *International*, Vol.3, No.4, Summer 1977, pp.13-17.
Rocard, M., *Michael Rocard Speaks: An Interview with Andrée Hoyles*, Spokesman Offprints No.13, 1974.
Seale, P. and McConville, M., *French Revolution 1968*, Penguin, 1968.
Singer, D., *Prelude to Revolution: France in May 1968*, London, 1970.
Strachey, J., *What Are We to Do?*, Left Book Club, 1938.
Therborn, G., 'The Rule of Capital and the Rise of Democracy', *New Left Review* 103, May-June 1977, pp.3-41.
Trotsky, L., *History of the Russian Revolution*, 3 Vols., Sphere 1967.
Trotsky, L., *The Struggle Against Fascism in Germany*, Pelican, 1976.
Trotsky, L., *1905*, Pelican, 1973.
Trotsky, L., *Writings on Britain*, 3 Vols., New Park, 1976.
Trotsky, L., 'The Transitional Programme', in *Documents of the Fourth International*, Pathfinder, 1973, pp.180-220.
Trotsky, L., *Writings 1938-9*, Merit, 1969.
Warren, W., 'Working Class Power: Britain's Crisis', *Problems of*

*Communism,* Winter 1977, British and Irish Communist Organisation, pp.17-35.

Warren, W. and Prior, M., *Advanced Capitalism and Backward Socialism,* Spokesman Pamphlet, 1975.

Watt, R.M., *The Kings Depart,* Pelican, 1973.

Williams, S., 'Trotskyism and Democracy', *The Guardian,* 22 January 1977.

Woodhouse, M. and Pearce, B., *Essays on the History of Communism in Britain,* New Park, 1975.

Since the bulk of this book was written two works have appeared, contents of which correspond to some of the major arguments in this book:

Miliband, R., *Marxism and Politics,* Oxford, 1977, esp. ch.6.

Poulantzas, N., 'The State and the Transition to Socialism' (Interview with H. Weber), in *International,* Vol.4, No.1, Autumn 1977.

12. Class basis of State.
34. Parliament & Collective Bargaining.
42. Lessons of failure of rev in Germany.
55. Miliband - dual perspective Parl & extra Parl struggle!
56. Women & E.P.A... & Parliament.
57. Planning agreements... & Workers Control.
74 Bennism.
100. Milliband on Parl "transition to socialism."
112. Civil Society & State - Anderson.
122. Anderson & Kautsky.
123. Govt Supporting revolution. see 129.